Teacher-Tested Classroom Management Strategies

Second Edition

Blossom S. Nissman, Ed.D.

Upper Saddle River, New Jersey
Columbus, Ohio

Vice President and Executive Publisher: Jeffrey W. Johnston
Executive Editor: Debra A. Stollenwerk
Production Editor: Alexandrina B. Wolf
Design Coordinator: Diane C. Lorenzo
Cover Designer: Ali Mohrman
Cover Image: Eyewire
Production Manager: Susan Hannahs
Director of Marketing: Ann Castel Davis
Marketing Manager: Darcy Betts Prybella
Marketing Coordinator: Brian Mounts

This book was set in Times Roman by Pearson Education, Inc. It was printed and bound by Courier Stoughton, Inc. The cover was printed by Courier Stoughton, Inc.

Pearson Education Ltd.
Pearson Education Singapore Pte. Ltd.
Pearson Education Canada, Ltd.
Pearson Education—Japan

Pearson Education Australia Pty. Limited
Pearson Education North Asia Ltd.
Pearson Educación de Mexico, S.A. de C.V.
Pearson Education Malaysia Pte. Ltd.

10 9 8 7 6 5 4 3 2 1
ISBN 0-13-171509-7

To my grandchildren:
Christopher and Danielle Nissman
Kelsey and Kendall Young

Whose bright and creative minds, love of learning, and enthusiasm for the joys of each day provide me with confidence and hope as they prepare to build a safe and productive world of tomorrow.

To their parents:
Karen and David Nissman
Debbi and Michael Young

Who continue to provide their children with a loving, supportive home that encourages them to become the best they can be

To my sister Faith S. Kurtzberg
Who is always ready to listen and encourage me with patience, understanding, and wisdom

PREFACE

This booklet was developed in response to pre-school to high school teachers' concerns regarding classroom management, as well as productive relationships with administration, colleagues, parents, and communities. (For ease of reading, "he" represents both male and female persons throughout the booklet.)

Teachers who have successfully responded to classroom management problems reviewed the identified concerns. Descriptors of their successful techniques are presented. It is important to note that although a solution or suggestion may seem applicable to a lower grade level, the procedure can be modified with slight variations to effectively respond to the older student. Techniques suggested for the higher grades can also be modified to respond to the needs of younger students.

The management techniques listed under each topic are not presented in sequential order. Rather, they are listed randomly as provided by the teachers so that the reader can choose the procedure that is most effective with his students. It can be likened to a "smorgasbord" of ideas from which the teacher can select the "tastiest morsel" as "food for thought!" The teacher can then hone them to perfection so they work for the class and/or for an individual student. In addition, successful and original elementary classroom and secondary management programs are presented and provide the reader with suggested guidelines for implementing these programs.

This booklet will assist and encourage innovation in teaching and presents management methods that will give the classroom teacher the freedom to provide each child with maximum opportunities to learn. Those of us who worked diligently on this project sincerely hope that our efforts will enhance the instructional quality of the classrooms of those who use the ideas and suggestions presented.

New to This Edition

- Additional *Workable Options* have been added throughout the booklet and continue to serve as possible solutions to classroom management issues

- Specific management suggestions from middle and secondary teachers in **Section III**

- A suggested management system for middle/secondary level students through the introduction of the *Motivational Theory* concept in **Section IV**, in addition to suggestions dealing with management problems specifically identified in middle/secondary schools

- The role of the school guidance counselor with respect to classroom management and discipline in **Section V**

- Concluding comments addressed directly to beginning teachers

- An expanded and current list of **Additional Resources**

A Caveat

Certain terms that may not be familiar to the reader because of their locale, or because they use another term to explain the same service, are found in this text.

- Child Study Team (CST) is the term used in many states for the professional staff within school districts who work cooperatively to determine the classification of students needing special academic or behavioral assistance in their classroom performance.

  The CST includes the cooperative meeting of the *School Psychologist* who completes the psychological study of the child; *the Social Worker* who is involved with the home and family; the *Teacher Consultant* who reports the findings of the team and works directly with the classroom teacher to develop the student's Individual Educational Plan (IEP); and the *classroom teacher(s)* who work directly with the student and his parents or guardians.

  The members of the Child Study Team collate the results of their individual information and use this material to develop the IEP. This is an ongoing process that is reviewed annually. Occasionally the School Administrator may be involved in determining the placement of the student or the program suggested by the CST.

- **Sociogram** refers to the process of having students respond to questions involving their relationships in the classroom, which helps them develop healthy interpersonal relationships with their peers. Details can be found in any book dealing with the basics of psychology and group interaction.

When using this booklet as a resource, keep in mind that the welfare of the student is the primary concern. These techniques are effective when used with moderation and as an integral part of the classroom curriculum. The classroom climate needs to reflect sensitivity through positive interpersonal relationships. This, in turn, helps foster a relaxed atmosphere that will instill confidence in the students making them emotionally equipped and actively involved in the learning process.

Acknowledgments

I would like to acknowledge the past contributions and guidance of Dr. Martin L. Stamm, Professor Emeritus of the College of New Jersey, who was involved in the original project and contributed a great deal to the professional quality of this publication.

I would also like to recognize the following contributors for their hard work and dedication in helping me make this second edition richer and more meaningful for beginning teachers:

First edition: Candice Bradley, Mary Ann Klicka, John Misieczko, Carrie Rudolph, and Steven Rosenbloom

Second edition: Amy Bush, Jane Corley, Mark Dale, Philip DeMara, S. Eliott-Walkes, Marie Hart, Clare Huggins, April Jamison, Kathy Koch, Carol McLarney, Linda Newpoint, Michelle Newman, Kristy Raber, Belle Shields, Melissa Shinn, Patricia Weis, Julie Williamson, and Loralee Wilt

Heartfelt thanks and special recognition go to Beryl McKintosh, Dr. Harlene Galen, and Dr. Don Lucas who encouraged their staff to be active participants by sharing their successful classroom management experiences.

Blossom S. Nissman, Ed.D.
drblossom@comcast.net
Professor of Education, Georgian Court University, NJ
Administrator, Long Beach Island Consolidated Schools, NJ
Director, 10 District School Consortium, Burlington County, NJ
Elementary School Counselor, Willingboro, NJ
Elementary School Teacher, Pennsylvania School Districts

TABLE OF CONTENTS

SECTION II

A TEACHER-TESTED ELEMENTARY CLASSROOM
MANAGEMENT SYSTEM   111

SECTION V

THE SCHOOL COUNSELOR'S ROLE IN CLASSROOM MANAGEMENT   **143**

SECTION VI

CONCLUSION AND ADDITIONAL RESOURCES   **147**

SECTION I

CLASSROOM MANAGEMENT STRATEGIES

Note: Readers will find instances where the **MANAGEMENT PROBLEM** and **WORKABLE OPTIONS** may be relevant at both elementary and middle/secondary levels.

MANAGEMENT PROBLEM:	*ABSENTEEISM/ATTENDANCE # 1*

TEACHER'S CONCERN:

What can I do in order to deal more effectively with students who are absent excessively for any number of reasons (e.g., illnesses, family responsibilities, or school phobias)?

WORKABLE OPTIONS:

1. Reinforce students whenever they attend school with a special activity and/or event of their own choosing (e.g., ten minutes of talking with classmates)

2. Provide individual conferences for those students who are fearful of school (e.g., anxiety about failure).

3. Have the student role play the feared situation in the presence of the teacher. After rehearsing alternative ways of responding to the student's fear, try several actual everyday situations.

4. Contact parents to find out why the student isn't regularly attending school. (In some cases, duties at home have a higher priority than school attendance.)

5. Place the student who is frequently absent in a group with two other students whom he is friends with and who come to school regularly. Tell him that his regular attendance will earn points for the group. At the end of the week, those points can be exchanged for a special activity of the group's choosing.

6. Send home class and/or homework assignments via friends, relatives, and personal phone calls so that the student doesn't fall behind the rest of the class.

7. Individualize instruction for those students who have returned to school after a long period of absence so that they will not fall behind the rest of the class.

8. Refer the student who is continually absent to the appropriate supportive school personnel (counselor, attendance officer, nurse, etc.)

MANAGEMENT PROBLEM:	*ABSENTEEISM/ATTENDANCE # 2*

TEACHER'S CONCERN: How can I get better attendance in the classes I teach?

WORKABLE OPTIONS:

1. Get in touch with the family to discuss the problem.

2. Provide the student with activities that are open-ended and need follow up so he feels a responsibility to come to school the next day.

3. Make instruction meaningful to the student.

4. Reward the student if absenteeism decreases.

5. Discuss with the student the reason why he is absent.

6. Give the student responsibility in the classroom that demands daily attention. Help him understand that his absence will handicap group progress. On the elementary level, it could be a responsibility to lead the line to the cafeteria or to feed the class pet. On the secondary level, it could involve work with a specific group on a project.

7. End the day with a "cliff hanger," an open-ended query that will be discussed the next day or the next session for secondary students. The students then become actively involved in finding the resolution and realize that their contributions and their attendance is vital.

8. Recognize and acknowledge student participation daily. A good work list in a conspicuous place in the classroom on a bulletin board, changed weekly, clearly defines the importance of attendance.

| MANAGEMENT PROBLEM: | *ADJUSTING TO SCHOOL ROUTINES* |

MANAGEMENT PROBLEM: *ADJUSTING TO SCHOOL ROUTINES*

TEACHER'S CONCERN: How can I help students adjust to the routine of the school day?

WORKABLE OPTIONS:

1. While sitting in a circle with students, ask them to share their ideas of favorite activities in school. This information can be used to set up the routine.

2. In small groups, ask students to share their feelings about their daily routine on a monthly basis. Choose a group leader (alternate leaders each week) and discuss with the group changes they could make to improve their choices and situations. Have them share these suggestions with the entire class.

3. Post the daily routine of the classroom on a bulletin board.

4. Establish a game called "rabbit." Students who follow the daily routine and get their work done receive a paper rabbit on their desks.

5. On a weekly basis, evaluate the students and discuss with them their adjustment to the school routine.

6. For younger students, provide a break (such as a fruit break) between morning academic sessions.

7. Make every effort to be consistent in classroom routines. Students often have difficulty when too many changes are made; they therefore cannot give their full concentration to the lesson.

8. Be prepared for the lesson planned with appropriate tools on hand (e.g., pencils, pens, etc.) for those students that need them. Often too much work time is lost because of the few students who are unprepared. Handle that problem later, rather than delaying the lesson at the expense of the rest of the class.

MANAGEMENT PROBLEM:	*AFTER-SCHOOL JOB INTEREST RESULTS IN ACADEMIC PROBLEMS*

TEACHER'S CONCERN: A student's academic performance is dropping as a result of his after-school job. How can I help students maintain an acceptable level of achievement?

WORKABLE OPTIONS:

1. Ask his parents to limit the number of hours that he can work (e.g., reduce a seven- hour day to three hours). Source: Cole, S. "Send Our Children to Work." *Psychology Today*, July 1997, 14 (2), p. 68.

2. Recommend to the parents that he be allowed to work only on weekends.

3. If the student is failing several courses, encourage him to take a leave of absence from work until his grades are acceptable.

4. Talk to the employer about the problem and request that he urge the student to keep up with his schoolwork.

5. Provide individual conferences with the student to discuss his academic responsibilities. Discuss the student's priorities and actual need for earnings.

6. Suggest an in-school cooperative education program to the student and parents. (The student may need more structure and support.)

7. Propose a vocational school to the student and parents.

8. Refer the student to the school guidance counselor.

9. Use parental and/or administrative pressure on the student when all other options have been exhausted.

MANAGEMENT PROBLEM:	*ALCOHOL USE*
TEACHER'S CONCERN:	A student comes to class inebriated. What should I do?
WORKABLE OPTIONS:	

1. Immediately send the student to the principal's office and have him detained until you can talk to him.

2. Notify parents of the student's condition.

3. Ask the school psychologist and/or guidance counselor to talk to the student.

4. Seek administrative support in this matter. Refer to your teacher's manual for the procedure to be followed.

5. Follow up on referrals on a daily basis.

6. If the student has been suspended from school, contact the parents and inquire about the student.

7. Remind students periodically about the school's policy regarding drinking.

8. Provide private follow-up conferences with the student to discuss his reasons for drinking.

9. Check the school manual or handbook concerning the procedure determined by the Board of Education for responding to this situation.

10. Confiscate any alcohol found in the student's possession and give it to the appropriate staff dealing with this situation.

MANAGEMENT PROBLEM:	*ANNOYING CLASSROOM DISTRACTIONS*

TEACHER'S CONCERN: How can a teacher prevent irritating classroom behaviors?

WORKABLE OPTIONS:

1. Have the students and teacher first discuss and then write a "group" contract adopting acceptable classroom rules and procedures by the end of the first week of school.

2. Periodically review the rules and procedures of the classroom until the students can successfully adhere to them.

3. Use simple verbal reprimands when the misbehavior occurs. Make sure that they are to the point, moderate in tone, and private (e.g., "Stop talking and work on your math problems, please.")

4. Give praise to the entire class as frequently as possible (e.g., "Thank you for working so quietly" or "I'm delighted to see you all working so well today.")

5. A student who continually exhibits an unacceptable behavior (e.g., out of seat) might profit from an "individualized" contract pinpointing the "desired" behavior (e.g., remaining in his seat) and delineating the consequences (e.g., if goal is reached, then student will receive designated reward or recognition).

6. Intervene as soon as possible in order to prevent the misbehavior from occurring (e.g., "Harry, may I help you with your assignment?" as the student begins to show signs of frustration).

7. Use facial expressions to convey to the student that the misbehavior was not totally overlooked. Circulate around the room frequently to avert potential behavior problems.

MANAGEMENT PROBLEM:	*ANTAGONISM WITH AUTHORITY*

TEACHER'S CONCERN:

What can I do to help students improve their interaction with authority figures?

WORKABLE OPTIONS:

1. Provide opportunities for students to change their hostile and aggressive energy into socially acceptable channels such as sports, clubs, crafts, hobbies, etc.

2. Give students reading and/or writing assignments that deal with antagonistic behaviors and ask them to comment on different socially acceptable ways of handling conflict situations.

3. Praise the students whenever they are cooperating with other adults (e.g., "That was very kind of you to help her find her keys").

4. Talk to the student in private to ascertain the reason for his misbehavior.

5. Provide the students with models of appropriate communicative behavior through role-playing activities.

6. Encourage students to strive for greater self-control in as many situations as possible.

7. Emphasize to the students the difference that exists between acceptable communication in school and those that are used at home and/or in the community.

8. Contact parents and/or administrators when there is no other way of resolving the conflict situation.

9. Refer the student to the appropriate members of the Child Study Team (see clarification of CST in Section 1) if he or she frequently displays uncontrollable verbal hostility. Keep anecdotal records to support your concerns.

MANAGEMENT PROBLEM:	*ARGUMENTATIVE STUDENT*
TEACHER'S CONCERN:	How do I deal with a child who becomes argumentative upon confrontation?

WORKABLE OPTIONS:

1. Do not confront the student in a group situation.

2. Do not use an accusatory tone upon approaching the student.

3. Evaluate the situation that led to the confrontation.

4. Do not back the student or yourself into a corner. Leave room for options.

5. Do not make threats that cannot be carried out.

6. Allow your emotions to cool before approaching the student.

7. Maintain an appearance of control at all times. Use a clear, firm voice.

8. Allow the child to have the opportunity to speak his side of the situation.

9. Allow for role-playing with role reversal. Role-playing is a technique that allows students to act out their interpretation of a problem and its solution. The entire class is given an opportunity for input and is less threatening than the teacher's demand for change.

10. Try to explore and discover what led to the confrontation and avoid repeating these circumstances.

11. If you made an error, admit it!

MANAGEMENT PROBLEM:	*ATTENTION-GETTING BEHAVIOR*

TEACHER'S CONCERN: What do I do about a student who exhibits attention-getting behavior?

WORKABLE OPTIONS:

1. Examine the cause of the behavior. Is it due to poor self-concept or being ignored, or is there a potential learning disability? Follow up on what you discover with appropriate school personnel.

2. Examine your reaction to the behavior and then change it if your behavior triggers a negative response.

3. Role-play. Give students a situation and have them play out acceptable and unacceptable behavior.

4. Discuss privately with the student the inappropriate behavior.

5. Ignore the behavior, if possible, so it cannot be used as an attention-getter.

6. Set up class rules in the beginning of the year and be consistent in enforcing them (Cantor's Assertive Discipline program, for example)

7. Use various modalities when giving directions. Write as well as say the assignment so all understand. Give examples and check the student's progress by moving around the room.

8. Examine your task assignments. Are they too difficult for some students? Are they clear? Be flexible. Change. Modify when necessary.

9. Give an abundance of praise. Student will strive for positive reinforcement from the teacher.

10. Attach consequences to the undesirable attention- getting behavior. Keep an accurate record of when each occurs for objective evaluation.

| **MANAGEMENT PROBLEM:** | *ATTENTION-SEEKING WELL-BEHAVED STUDENT* |

| **TEACHER'S CONCERN:** | What can I do with a child who is constantly seeking attention? |

WORKABLE OPTIONS:

1. Explain to the child that he is an important person, but that other individuals and/or the entire class also need your attention. Continue to give individual attention to this child whenever feasible, but slowly reduce it until it is equal to the amount you normally spend with a student.

2. There may be problems that you are unaware of, so the child should receive the services of the Child Study Team and the school counselor. The child will then get additional individual attention that may solve his problem.

3. If the child is from a single-parent family, you can, with the appropriate permission, recommend a "Big Brother or Sister" affiliation.

4. Often the attention-seeking child is a loner in the classroom. Carefully select another student to be his or her classroom "buddy." They are to do their assignments together as much as possible. This may fulfill the needs of the child and give the teacher more time for the other children. An appropriate "buddy" can be determined through a class sociogram. A sociogram is a technique that explores student interaction to one another; when used correctly, can unite students in a cooperative, productive way. (Details and procedures can be found in any text dealing with educational psychology.)

5. Inform the parent(s) of the student's problem. Hopefully they will give the child more attention at home and alert you of any concerns that may relate to his need to seek attention in school.

MANAGEMENT PROBLEM:	*ATTITUDE CHANGE*

TEACHER'S CONCERN: Some students have a bad attitude. No matter what I do, they cannot be motivated. How do I get them to change?

WORKABLE OPTIONS:

1. Ignore his attitude but not his behavior. Do not let the student's negative attitude bother you. Discuss personally with the student your concerns.

2. Examine and change, if possible, the classroom environment. Make it brighter and cheerier. Use the interest of the students to decorate the room with their quality work and ideas.

3. Examine and adjust your teaching style. Are you too tense, sober, callous, demanding, and sarcastic? Try to be more pleasant and excited about what you are teaching. Add humor and personalize your interaction with your students.

4. Plan your day so that "fun" things (activities that require movement and communication) occur between "work" periods.

5. Strive to present more chances for successful experiences to the student with the bad attitude. Give him earned and honest praise and encouragement at every opportunity.

6. Discuss with the class their plans for the future. Incorporate their career interests in your lessons. If students see the connection between what they are learning and their future, they are more apt to be self-motivated.

7. Discuss with the class the importance of a positive attitude. Present situations and have members of the class role play characters with and without good attitudes in varying real-life situations.

MANAGEMENT PROBLEM: *BATHROOM SHARING*

TEACHER'S CONCERN: How can one bathroom be shared when there are a large number of students in the classroom?

WORKABLE OPTIONS:

Classroom Bathrooms

1. Discuss with your students the necessity for sharing the bathroom.

2. Set up a bathroom schedule.

3. Prior to lunch, when the use of the bathroom is more frequent, allow students to use the bathroom upon completion of assignments.

4. Set specific time limits on stay in the bathroom.

5. Refer any constant user to the school nurse in the event that a medical problem exists.

6. Use a rotating sign on the bathroom door to indicate if the bathroom is occupied or unoccupied.

7. Never use the forbidden use of the bathroom as punishment.

Hall Bathrooms

1. Clearly define bathroom rules from the first day of class.

2. Stress courtesy.

3. See rules above.

4. Provide a bathroom pass or sign out sheet with time noted so extended time (and mischief) in the bathroom is avoided.

MANAGEMENT PROBLEM:	*BEHAVIOR PROBLEMS*
TEACHER CONCERN:	What is a simple but good discipline technique to resolve a student's constant misbehavior?
WORKABLE OPTIONS:	When a child exhibits unacceptable behavior, follow the steps listed below:

1. If possible, meet with the child and describe in exact terms the behavior you find unacceptable in the classroom.

2. During the discussion, explain the reason(s) that you find the behavior unacceptable.

3. Be sure the child understands that it is not he who is unacceptable but rather the behavior.

4. Let the student know exactly what will happen if the problem continues.

5. If the misbehavior occurs again, follow through with the previously planned disciplinary action.

6. Throughout the process, keep the parents and the principal informed of the progress or lack of progress.

7. If the child continues to misbehave and you feel that you have utilized all of your options and resources, send the child to the appropriate disciplinary office or person in the school. Explain to the child that he is welcome to return when he is ready to follow the classroom rules.

8. If the misbehavior is through note passing (especially common among teenage girls), confiscate the note but do not read it. Put it away for the moment, then return it privately to the student while discussing its inappropriateness.

MANAGEMENT PROBLEM:	*BOASTFUL, ATTENTION-SEEKING STUDENT*

TEACHER'S CONCERN:

What can I do for students who are constantly disrupting the class in order to gain my attention? (See *Attention-Getting Behavior* and *Attention-Seeking, Well-Behaved Student,* pp. 11-12.)

WORKABLE OPTIONS:

1. Give the student a position of responsibility in the classroom and encourage him to set a good example for others (e.g., passing out papers).

2. Post a chart in the front of the room delineating the rules to be followed when responding (e.g., raise your hand if you wish to talk; wait to be called on; listen while others talk, etc.).

3. Assign the student a special project of interest and have him present his report to the class.

4. Ignore the student's annoying comments but praise him when he tells of his real achievements.

5. Assign the student to a small group in which he must primarily participate as a follower.

6. Provide frequent recognition and positive attention whenever possible.

7. Model appropriate behavior every day for the student so that he can see what is expected of him (e.g., role playing by teacher and/or peers).

8. Arrange parent conferences to discuss any factors that may be contributing to the student's problem in school (e.g., sibling rivalry).

MANAGEMENT PROBLEM:	*BULLETIN BOARDS*

TEACHER'S CONCERN:	Bulletin boards can help with classroom management. How can changing bulletin boards be made less time consuming?

WORKABLE OPTIONS:

1. Maintain one bulletin board throughout the year for school menus, bulletins, calendars, and honor lists. Little change is needed in such an arrangement.

2. Designate one bulletin board for student work only. Appoint student helpers to post student work worthy of display.

3. Incorporate the making of a bulletin board scene as part of a lesson. Many learning skills are involved in such an activity.

4. Designate one bulletin board in the classroom for which the students are responsible. Appoint teams to design and change the scenes and displays when necessary.

5. Use the bulletin board for an exchange of information. Make an "I Want to Know" board. Students write questions for which they would like answers; other students are responsible for researching and supplying the answers.

6. See extensive suggestions on this topic in *New Dimensions in Elementary Guidance* by Martin L. Stamm and Blossom S. Nissman (New York: Richards Rosen Press, 1971).

7. See Section III for further details on effective use of bulletin boards at the secondary level.

MANAGEMENT PROBLEM:	*CALLING OUT IN CLASS—RESPONSE #1*
TEACHER'S CONCERN:	What can I do with a student who calls out answers or comments during class?

WORKABLE OPTIONS:

1. Discuss your expectations with the class. Make up rules and consequences at the very beginning of the school year.

2. Keep a frequency record in your grade book of the calling out and increase the severity of the consequence in direct proportion to its frequency.

3. With children in the middle grades and older, divide the class into two groups and make a game out of questions and answers. Each team scores a point for each correct answer. If a team member calls out an answer out of turn, that team loses a set amount of points.

4. Praise the student who does not call out but waits to be called on.

5. Ignore the calling out. Do not acknowledge having heard it.

6. Use a strict behavior modification program to lessen and ultimately extinguish this behavior.

7. Examine the reason for calling out. Is it for attention? Do you overlook calling on this student? Is it a result of inability to sit still? Does this child have a learning disability? React to these symptoms appropriately.

8. Contact the parents. Try an at-home reward system for good days when he did not call out. This will involve sending a daily note home.

MANAGEMENT PROBLEM:	*CALLING OUT IN CLASS—RESPONSE # 2*

TEACHER'S CONCERN: I am extremely frustrated by children constantly calling out in class even when they are supposed to be working quietly at their seats. What can I do about it?

WORKABLE OPTIONS:

1. Be sure that the students are aware of what you expect of them concerning this problem. Instead of calling out in class, explain the procedure that you want them to use to get your attention, and the reason for it.

2. If students' calling out is a major problem, have a class meeting. Have the children make recommendations to solve this problem, including the type of discipline to be used for the children who continue to disturb the class.

3. Be consistent and persistent in disciplining the children who call out.

4. If a child communicates with you by calling out, make your only reaction one of displeasure and do not answer the question or fulfill the request.

5. Tell the class that if calling out in class only occurs a certain amount of times during the week, you will do something special with them on Friday afternoon. Peer pressure is then utilized in solving the problem. Lower the number of times calling out in class each week in order to receive the special Friday activity.

6. Calling out may be motivated by enthusiasm or the fear that he will forget what he wanted to say. Have students keep a pad and pencil on their desk to write down their thoughts so they can refer to it when they finally get called upon. Be sure to give everyone a chance to answer something, even the slower-thinking students!

MANAGEMENT PROBLEM:	*CHILDREN FROM BROKEN HOMES*

TEACHER'S CONCERN: How can I help the student during the separation and/or divorce of his parents?

WORKABLE OPTIONS:

1. If the student shows no signs of being affected by this experience, respect his privacy and do not bring the issue to his attention.

2. If the student wants to talk, be an attentive listener but do not pry, take sides, or discuss information you have heard or learned from others.

3. Do not rationalize the child's changed behavior as understandable because his parents are having problems. Be sure that is the reason and then handle accordingly using the guidance and Child Study Team services available in your school.

4. Consider contacting one or both parents if there is significant change in the student's academic, social, or emotional behavior.

5. Have a small group session with several children in your class who have already experienced this within their homes.

6. Often, children feel a sense of responsibility when a separation takes place or there is disruption at home. Give this student balance and an improved sense of self-worth by giving him responsibility in the classroom that requires his leadership.

7. Do not play "marriage counselor." Be noncommittal in regard to the pros and cons of divorce. Be supportive of whatever living arrangements are made and if the child is to remain in your class, show your pleasure. If he is moved to another location and will be leaving you, encourage this move with positive support.

MANAGEMENT PROBLEM:	*CLASS CLOWN*

TEACHER'S CONCERN: How do I deal effectively with a "class clown"?

WORKABLE OPTIONS:

1. Let the student know in private how you feel about his unacceptable behavior and what is expected of him. Try to form a trusting relationship. Listen to his feelings and expectations. Try to channel his talent for humor in a more productive vein, such as a class play or dramatic skit.

2. If you think it would be beneficial, do role-playing with this student. Give him the role of the teacher with a specific objective to teach during a lesson. You take the role of the class clown and exhibit the same behaviors that he does. This may be a learning experience for the entire class!

3. Explain to the student that the solution to his problem is both his and your responsibility. However, if the "class clown" behavior continues and it affects the level of learning for the rest of the class, then the responsibility for the solution will lie with him and the administration.

4. Try to find the curriculum areas in which the student is interested. Give him some independent work in this area and observe any change in behavior.

5. Let the child gain the attention of the class in such a way that it has a positive effect on the class. The student could conduct mini lessons, lead study groups, assist students, or make other contributions that benefit the entire class.

6. Ask a counselor to investigate various possible reasons for the child's need to be the "class clown."

MANAGEMENT PROBLEM:	*CLASSROOM RULES*

TEACHER'S CONCERN: What should I do when clear rules are set up in September, yet constant repetition of these rules is necessary for the student to follow them?

WORKABLE OPTIONS:

1. In establishing class rules, make the list as short as possible. The fewer the rules you must enforce, the fewer disciplinary actions you have to take.

2. Make the class rules relevant by ensuring that all the class rules are firmly based on educational considerations.

3. Make the rules meaningful and share the logical relationship to the educational tasks at hand.

4. Make the list positive. A positive statement offers a goal to work toward rather than a veiled threat to avoid.

5. Establish the consequences if a rule is broken. List the classroom rules in a prominent position on a bulletin board or the blackboard.

6. Pay attention to students who are on task and behaving appropriately by praising good behavior.

7. Reinforce positive responses to rules, such as a student following a class rule by raising his hand instead of calling out an answer. Reinforce this with the positive response of "Thank you, John, for raising your hand to answer that question!"

8. Make a copy of the rules and distribute to all the students.

9. On a weekly basis, have a short conference with each offending student. Relate how they have followed the rules that week and agree on successes, needs for change, and ideas for improvement in class routine.

MANAGEMENT PROBLEM:	*CLEANING UP WORK AREAS*

TEACHER'S CONCERN: How can I teach children to clean work areas when they have finished using them?

WORKABLE OPTIONS:

1. Establish clean-up rules at the beginning of the year.

2. Show the students where things belong.

3. Establish class guidelines on classroom order.

4. Have them practice cleaning up.

5. Allow younger students more practice time than older ones.

6. Be consistent. Insist on cleaning up each time.

7. Provide adequate time for clean up. Plan for it.

8. Emphasize neatness and cleanliness whenever possible during the day by praising students.

9. Get students excited. Use shaving cream, which acts as a great cleaning tool and is fun to use.

10. Do not allow students who do not clean up to use work areas for a period of time.

11. Use a bell or some other signal to signify clean-up time. As soon as students hear or see this signal, they are to begin cleaning up.

12. Make a "Success Day" chart. List clean-up as one success to be accomplished. Mark charts at the end of each day.

13. Make a checklist of clean-up tasks. Attach to each work area.

14. Appoint student helpers to monitor peers.

MANAGEMENT PROBLEM:	*CLERICAL WORK*

TEACHER'S CONCERN: How can I incorporate clerical duties into the daily management of the classroom (lunch money collection, attendance, paper filing, etc.)?

WORKABLE OPTIONS:

1. Appoint student helpers to collect money and to fill out daily forms.

2. Copy a list of your students' names. Leave room for several boxes next to each name. Use these forms to expedite collecting or counting procedures. Example:

Name	*Lunch*	*Attendance*	*Homework*
John	no	yes	yes

3. To help make money collection easier and more accurate, assign each child an envelope with his name on it. Children put their money into these envelopes and close them. Have a student helper collect the envelopes and place them in a box.

4. To expedite the filing of papers, enlist your class as helpers. A variety of learning skills are involved in this procedure.

5. Follow a consistent routine so the students feel comfortable responding to your direction and are prepared to follow through on the materials you wish to collect, account for, etc.

6. Use a desk calendar to keep a record of what is due and when it is due so that you submit all reports and materials on time.

7. Check your teacher's manual carefully to determine how you order supplies, when you're responsible for bus duty, as well as other areas for which you are responsible.

MANAGEMENT PROBLEM:	*COMMUNICATION WITH THE ADMINISTRATION*

TEACHER'S CONCERN: Our building principal does not make himself available to assist in the daily problems that confront classroom teachers. What can we do about this?

WORKABLE OPTIONS:

1. Ask for a conference with the principal to honestly share your needs and see if it brings about a change.

2. If you feel uncomfortable about approaching the principal directly, send a note asking for his assistance in a particular situation and wait for a response. If there is no response, try the following procedures.

3. To solve certain types of problems, you may want to turn to individual faculty members who have taken on various leadership roles and whose professionalism you respect.

4. Many types of problems that face teachers daily can be alleviated by a staff member often overlooked—the custodian. He can be a tremendous resource, so develop a positive and functional relationship with him.

5. The faculty meeting between the teachers and administration may provide the opportunity to discuss such a problem.

6. As a new teacher, you have the "ear" and input of your mentor teacher. Be sure to take advantage of this source of information.

7. **Establish a respectful relationship with your school secretary. She is usually aware of the heartbeat of the school.**

MANAGEMENT PROBLEM:	*CONTROLLING OTHER CLASSROOM STUDENTS WHILE INSTRUCTING INDIVIDUALS OR SMALL GROUPS*

TEACHER'S CONCERN: How can I control students at their seats while I am providing individual or small group instruction?

WORKABLE OPTIONS:

1. Have various enrichment activities readied for students when they are finished with their assigned work. Make the selection of the enrichment activities part of your daily lesson plan.

2. Be sure that the students understand what behavior is expected of them during their independent work. Place these "rules" on a poster and place it in view of the class. If any rule needs to be discussed, it can easily be pointed to and presented to the class.

3. If there are a few students who continually disrupt the class while working independently, place them in isolated locations in the classroom (but never behind you in front of the room where they can perform for their peers outside your view). Explain to them that they can have their previous seats when they are ready to follow the classroom rules during independent work time.

4. Select competent students as resource persons within the classroom. When you are working with a group, these resource students can assist the rest of the class in answering basic questions and supplying needed materials during their independent work time.

5. Ask the principal if he can schedule you to observe a teacher on the staff who effectively deals with this particular management problem.

| MANAGEMENT PROBLEM: | *COPING WITH THE DEATH OF A RELATIVE, PEER, OR FRIEND OF A STUDENT* |

MANAGEMENT PROBLEM: *COPING WITH THE DEATH OF A RELATIVE, PEER, OR FRIEND OF A STUDENT*

TEACHER'S CONCERN: How can I aid a student who has lost a family member, a friend, or a fellow student?

WORKABLE OPTIONS:

1. Offer an open line of communication to the student by making him aware that you know of this sad event and would be willing to talk about it if he chooses.

2. Respond to the student's questions with honest and direct answers.

3. Keep in mind the child's age and his capacity to understand the enormity of the situation.

4. If a parent has died, try to communicate with the surviving parent and offer support in helping the child cope with the loss.

5. If a sibling or friend has died, a group discussion would be a reasonable approach. Through this discussion, students have the support of their peers and become quickly aware of the fact that they have common fears and concerns. The teacher leading this discussion must clearly avoid religious views and maudlin attitudes. A sense of concern and caring should permeate the discussion.

6. Allow time for the student to get back into the routine of school. Involve the school counselor and any other school services if you think that the child seems depressed or confused.

7. Recommend to the parent(s) a free copy of *Caring About Kids: Talking to Children About Death,* available from Public Inquiries, National Institute of Mental Health, 5600 Fishers Lane, Rockville, MD 20857.

MANAGEMENT PROBLEM:	*CURSING*

TEACHER'S CONCERN: What do I do when a student curses at a teacher or a fellow student in the classroom?

WORKABLE OPTIONS:

1. Ignore it if it will become a central point in the classroom. Privately work with the child to discuss the offense.

2. Examine the causes of such language. Is it anger or habit? If it's in anger, work on teaching the student socially-acceptable forms of expressing anger. Suggest alternatives for coping with stress.

3. Role-play or discuss socially acceptable ways of showing anger.

4. Initiate a behavior modification program to change habitual cursing.

5. Attach a consequence. Make sure the severity of the consequence is in direct proportion to the frequency of the cursing. Keep an accurate record, preferably in the back of the pupil's record book, of when the infraction happens so you can anticipate and prevent it.

6. Discuss the advantages of proper language. Provide word games in class, introducing new and sophisticated vocabulary to spark interest in alternate verbal expression.

7. Contact the parents. Get an idea of how they feel about this and enlist their support. Help them establish a reward system for days in which the frequency of cursing is diminished and subsequently eliminated.

8. Clearly make the point that cursing is not acceptable in school.

9. If this behavior persists, refer the student to the school disciplinarian according to your Board policy or rules in the Teachers' Manual.

MANAGEMENT	
PROBLEM:	*DAYDREAMING*

TEACHER'S
CONCERN: How can I help a child who is constantly daydreaming?

WORKABLE
OPTIONS:

1. If the student frequently exhibits this type of behavior, he should be referred to the Child Study Team to investigate possible causes. There may be a serious medical problem involved.

2. When you notice the child daydreaming, check later to see if he did not understand the topic being discussed. If this is the case, then the problem is not daydreaming; instead, it is the child's lack of readiness in that particular subject area.

3. Make it a habit to ask the students questions during the teaching lesson. It will raise their attention level to know that at any time they must provide answers on the content of the lesson.

4. If you notice several students daydreaming, then try to develop lessons in which the students are more involved with the learning experience.

5. Make daily involvement in the classroom activities part of each student's evaluation. Try to give the students weekly feedback that reflects their improvement in this area.

6. Move the child's seat so that looking out the window is not as inviting. Place him in the center of the classroom so he will feel like an integral member of the class.

7. Be sure the student is able to see and hear you clearly and does not have an impairment that prevents this. Ask the school nurse to check this out. If it continues, mention to the parents your concern and suggest a complete medical check-up.

MANAGEMENT PROBLEM:	*DEMANDING STUDENTS*

TEACHER'S CONCERN: How do I cope with a child who demands my constant attention?

WORKABLE OPTIONS:

1. Give the child a special job to show you care and have confidence in him.

2. Make the child captain or leader whenever possible.

3. Play games that nourish self-confidence. Circle game: Children try to name someone in the circle who has done something to help them or to make them feel good.

4. Use personal evaluation sheets. These can be as simple or as complex as you desire. This helps children express their feelings and see their strengths/weaknesses in a non-threatening atmosphere.

5. Provide a wide variety of classroom experiences. Familiarity breeds self-confidence.

6. Implement a buddy system for the child.

7. Check into the home environment. See what is motivating this dependency.

8. Provide the child with simple, easy to accomplish tasks that allow for frequent success.

9. Provide self-correcting tasks so that the child may see his own errors first-hand.

10. Videotape your class in action and let the student, as well as the other students, actually see how he interacts in class. (Be sure to acquire student permission to share this personal tape before showing it to the entire class.)

MANAGEMENT PROBLEM:	*DESTRUCTIVENESS TO PROPERTY*

TEACHER'S CONCERN: Some students show "carelessness" toward other people's personal and/or school property, while others are willfully destructive. How can I impede these aversive behaviors?

WORKABLE OPTIONS:

1. Try to make the punishment fit the crime (e.g., if a student breaks a pencil negligently, then it should be paid for or replaced if it was the school's property).

2. Demand that the student make some kind of mutually agreed upon retribution for his careless behavior.

3. Assign students who destroy school property to special "work" details in and around the school (e.g., repainting walls that have graffiti on them, picking up trash, cleaning up the cafeteria after a food fight, etc.).

4. Provide "constructive" classroom projects for students who get easily frustrated and/or overly anxious (e.g., build a classroom bookcase).

5. Give positive recognition and attention to these students when they are careful with other people's possessions and/or property (e.g., "That was very nice of you to pick up Susan's coat, Bill").

6. Contact parents and/or inform administration when no viable solution can be reached.

7. Inform the police, juvenile court authorities, and other outside supportive agencies if there is an obvious and continuing pattern of destructive behavior. Be sure to consult your Teachers' Handbook before initiating any outside help so that you follow the appropriate procedures.

MANAGEMENT PROBLEM:	*DEVELOPING LISTENING SKILLS*
TEACHER'S CONCERN:	How can I develop and improve students' listening skills?

WORKABLE OPTIONS:

1. Read to the class aloud and discuss details.

2. Play "What Did I Do?" Have children cover their eyes. Try sharpening a pencil, stirring a spoon in a bowl, etc.; then ask children what they have heard.

3. Take time to listen to environmental sounds. Take the children outside and have them listen to the noises they hear and jot them down in their "listening" tablet.

4. Tap out rhythms and have the children repeat what they heard.

5. Give simple verbal instructions for the children to follow.

6. Play "Whisper Down the Lane" where the first child in a line is told something and this must be passed down the line. Usually the last person's interpretation does not resemble the original message emphasizing the importance of good listening skills.

7. Play restaurant. Children give orders and try to repeat the orders.

8. Help children try to eliminate as many distractions as possible by recognizing distraction in the classroom (fish tank, other group discussions, etc.).

9. Play repeating games using words or numerals. Child makes the statement: "For lunch I had ____" and each child adds to the list by first repeating what he heard and then adding his contribution.

10. Ask the school nurse to check the hearing of those children who seem to have difficulty.

MANAGEMENT PROBLEM:	*DISRESPECT*
TEACHER'S CONCERN:	What can one do with a child who shows disrespect toward me and the other students in the class?
WORKABLE OPTIONS:	

1. An immediate approach is to inform the child that this type of behavior is unacceptable, then clearly explain the consequences if it occurs again.

2. Inform the parent(s) of the child's behavior and request their continual assistance in helping the child with this problem.

3. Have an individual conference with the child. Include the services of a counselor if it is available and have the child share his feelings concerning the problem and its possible solution.

4. Carefully select a child to team up with him in as many classroom activities and assignments as possible. Then, after a period of time, observe and evaluate any positive or negative change in the child.

5. A valuable experience in assisting a teacher with this and many other classroom problems is a course called "Teacher Effectiveness Training" or T.E.T. (Gordon). It shows you how to solve problems with students in the classroom without either person losing.

6. In order to gain respect, a teacher needs to model respect toward students, colleagues, and others in all situations. *Sarcasm* is the surest way to lose the respect of your students. *It is unprofessional and uncalled for under any circumstances.*

| MANAGEMENT PROBLEM: | *DISRUPTION IN LEARNING CAUSED BY STUDENT ATTENDANCE IN MANDATED PROGRAMS* |

MANAGEMENT PROBLEM: *DISRUPTION IN LEARNING CAUSED BY STUDENT ATTENDANCE IN MANDATED PROGRAMS*

TEACHER'S CONCERN: How do I cope with the student who is involved in so many special programs in school that he or she is always out of class?

WORKABLE OPTIONS:

1. Try to remember that as the classroom teacher you will not be able to do "everything" for such a child. It is frustrating and nearly impossible to set such a goal for yourself.

2. Talk with the administrator about your specific concern so that he is aware of the limitations being set upon you.

3. Talk to the Resource Room teacher to see if you are able to get help from such personnel.

4. Create an extra time slot at the end of the day to help these students with material missed.

5. Use student tutors from upper grades to help these students.

6. Tape record core material. Use this as a basis for a learning center.

7. Make up fact sheets. Arrange parental cooperation for mastery of these skills using the fact sheets as a guideline.

8. Establish a buddy system for these students.

9. Provide the special teacher with copies of your worksheets that he can use to work on with the student when he is not in class with you.

MANAGEMENT PROBLEM:	*DISRUPTIVE BEHAVIOR (FIGHTING, ARGUMENTS)*

TEACHER'S CONCERN: What do I do with students who cannot get along with other students and continually get into fights and arguments?

WORKABLE OPTIONS:

1. Evaluate the sources of frustration in the classroom that may contribute to a student getting into a fight. The student is influenced by the teacher, classmates, and the activities.

2. Check the type of discipline at home. Work with the parents to see if there can be some consistency.

3. In younger children, intervention only convinces the student that he will get attention for fighting. If the teacher attempts to direct these activities, the children will learn how to manage negative feelings more productively. See Glasser's "Reality Therapy" theory for specific guidelines on positive reinforcement.

4. Role play fighting situations and discuss what may happen if someone gets hurt, how to handle these situations more effectively, and how to avoid these situations as well as alternative actions.

5. Take a student aside who has been fighting to find out what may have caused the fight. Never confront the student in front of the class.

6. Try to sit down with the students involved in the fight and see if a solution can be worked out.

7. Treat the student with respect and dignity to encourage his sense of responsibility for his own actions.

8. When discipline is necessary, be fair and consistent.

MANAGEMENT PROBLEM:	*DRAWING ON DESK/SCHOOL PROPERTY*

TEACHER'S CONCERN: What do I do if a student is doing something other than his work, such as playing under or drawing on his desk?

WORKABLE OPTIONS:

1. Establish rules for proper behavior during periods when students are at their desks.

2. Reinforce positive behavior of students who work at their desk properly.

3. Check to see that students have sufficient amount of work to keep them on task.

4. Vary your lessons so that students remain interested.

5. Collect pencils and crayons when they are not being used in your lesson, or be sure students clear their desks in preparation for the next activity.

6. Use hands-on projects as much as possible.

7. During regular class, give the students the chance to draw creatively as an interpretation of something they have learned.

8. Provide an interest center with drawing materials.

MANAGEMENT PROBLEM:	*DRUG ABUSE*
TEACHER'S CONCERN:	What should I do when I suspect and/or witness students involved with illegal drugs?
WORKABLE OPTIONS:	

1. Follow the procedure delineated in your school handbook in regard to drug abuse.

2. Have the child evaluated completely by the Child Study Team in your district.

3. Have the parents come in for a conference to discuss the child's home environment.

4. Speak to the class about drug problems and come up with solutions on how to help the student cope within the classroom environment.

5. Set up goals with the child that should be met within a certain time schedule.

6. Let the child work with one or more students to build relationships within the class.

7. Reward the child for positive behavior.

8. Encourage the child every day, it possible.

9. If it is prescribed medication, be sure the school nurse is informed.

10. Investigate agencies available to assist you in learning more about the drug problem with students of the age you teach.

11. Talk with other teachers that have this child in class to determine if they have observed this problem, especially if the student denies it.

| MANAGEMENT PROBLEM: | *FAILURE TO ASK FOR HELP/ SHYNESS* |

MANAGEMENT PROBLEM: *FAILURE TO ASK FOR HELP/ SHYNESS*

TEACHER'S CONCERN: What do I do about a student who fails to ask for help on matters he does not fully understand in the curriculum or the classroom in general?

WORKABLE OPTIONS:

1. For various reasons, the student may not feel comfortable or confident about asking questions in certain classroom settings. Have an individual conference with the student to discuss the problem and develop possible solutions together.

2. If the student does not feel comfortable asking questions in the classroom setting, have him write the questions on a piece of paper or a 3×5 card. Then when time permits, meet with the child individually to review the questions or provide general answers to the class because others may have the same questions.

3. Utilize other students in the classroom as resource persons to meet with the student and offer assistance. The student may be more apt to ask for help from a peer than from the teacher.

4. Consider the option of having the child evaluated by the Child Study Team for a possible learning disability or a health problem (poor hearing, poor vision, etc.)

5. Check to see if the student exhibits this behavior in other classrooms. If he/she does not, you may want to focus on the way you relate to this student.

6. If available and practical, utilize the services of a counselor to assist the child in overcoming his reluctance to express himself in class.

7. Establish a chart listing all students and give recognition to those who ask questions in class. Emphasize that asking a question indicates intelligence, not stupidity.

| MANAGEMENT PROBLEM: | *FIGHTING: NOT GETTING ALONG, NAME CALLING, ETC.* |

MANAGEMENT PROBLEM: *FIGHTING: NOT GETTING ALONG, NAME CALLING, ETC.*

TEACHER'S CONCERN: What do I do with students who do not get along? These students exhibit behaviors such as fighting, name-calling, ridiculing, pushing, and shoving at every opportunity.

WORKABLE OPTIONS:

1. Build self-confidence. Many books, articles, and material gleaned from the Internet provide suggestions on what to do.

2. Use the "Magic Circle" technique or Glasser's "Reality Therapy," Cantor's "Assertive Discipline," or Skinner's "Behavior Modification" approaches.

3. Do role-playing on how to handle a conflict situation. One skit should deal with socially-acceptable behavior and another in correcting a socially-unacceptable situation.

4. Discuss the importance of getting along in school, at home, and later in the working world.

5. Present situations concerning conflict resolutions. Have students break into groups to brainstorm socially acceptable solutions.

6. Check through films or videos available in the area of education. Look for materials dealing with social growth and conflict management.

7. Ignore the student's behavior unless safety warrants your immediate attention. Speak to the student privately later.

8. If the student is physically assaulting another student, break up the confrontation and allow the upset student to be isolated until he has sufficiently "cooled off." Follow school policy and record the incident for further referral.

MANAGEMENT PROBLEM: *FRUSTRATION*

TEACHER'S CONCERN: How can I help a child deal with frustration after he has missed a part of a lesson due to illness or absence from the room for other reasons?

WORKABLE OPTIONS:

1. Use the expertise of special teachers in your school and try to determine what caused the frustration.

2. Discuss the problem with the student in private.

3. Provide the student with time-out to calm himself before returning to work. Available resources such as a quiet spot in the classroom or an interest corner with earphones and tapes are helpful.

4. Provide the student with a classroom tutor whom he can seek out to get information on the area of his frustration. If the child is "classified," a classroom tutor is required by law and should be made available.

5. Rather than wait until a problem arises, be sure that the behavior expected in regard to entering and being part of the classroom is clearly defined.

6. Make every effort to schedule the student's time out of the classroom for when the lessons are in the same academic area or do not apply to him. For example, a student going to a Resource Room for individualized instruction in reading should go during the class reading period rather than during an art or science lesson.

7. Use the game "Class Applause" to assist in coping with this concern. Have the students sit in a circle and concentrate on providing words of encouragement and affection for each other. Make sure that this student is included in the praise. Positive motivation and respect by peers is a real morale builder!

MANAGEMENT PROBLEM:	*HANDS-ON PROJECTS*

TEACHER'S CONCERN: How can I obtain "hands-on projects or materials" for the students in my classroom?

WORKABLE OPTIONS:

1. First, investigate the materials that may be located in your school. It is amazing what you can find in a storage room collecting dust. Ask the custodian, librarian, and principal about such materials and their possible location.

2. Consult with teachers who have more experience with such materials than you and your "mentor." They will have much to share with you.

3. Check the Internet, local museums, community libraries, and teacher supply stores for ideas.

4. Select "hands-on" material from catalogs and ask the administration to order them for you.

5. Take field trips and collect samples. Be creative and keep alert for free materials you can use.

6. Check out your county or state Educational Resource Materials Centers. In New Jersey it is called the EIC (Educational Improvement Center). These centers have samples of all varieties of curricular materials that you may borrow.

7. Send letters to major corporations to find out what materials they have available free of charge. Many businesses are very receptive to such requests.

8. Check out professional journals for materials and ideas (*The Instructor* and *New Teacher Advocate* published by Kappa Delta Pi, *Teacher Magazine,* etc.). Use your college library resources for ideas found through the Internet.

MANAGEMENT PROBLEM:	*HOME INFLUENCES*

TEACHER'S CONCERN: What do I do when home problems interfere with students being able to concentrate on schoolwork and activities?

WORKABLE OPTIONS:

1. If a student is from a dysfunctional home, make sure you give him a friendly greeting, letting him know you are glad to see him.

2. If possible, request a parent conference. Try to discuss the academic problems the student is having. Be sure to plan this meeting with the parent(s) early in the school year and stress how important it is to work together to provide the educational experience possible. Explain clearly that if the child comes to school regularly, is well rested, and has had breakfast, you will be able to provide a maximum learning environment in the classroom. Ask if there is any way you can assist in lessening the child's stress from home problems or even the parent's stress.

3. If the child is not receiving breakfast at home or is not dressed properly (e.g., warm for winter) for school, call upon the school or community resources. This includes checking for need of glasses or dentistry, which can affect the student's learning ability.

4. Use the services of the school counselor or the nurse as an open line of communication. Often these staff members have resources for clothes (local stores merchandise out of season) and glasses (local service groups, etc.).

5. Minimize demands on student in regard to home assignments that would cause him hardship.

6. Follow up the first parent conference by calling or sending home notes describing positive actions of the student. This will help the child's sense of self-worth and increase his incentive to do even better in your safe and secure classroom.

MANAGEMENT PROBLEM:	*HOMEWORK*

TEACHER'S CONCERN: What can I do to get more students to do their homework consistently?

WORKABLE OPTIONS:

1. When correcting homework, mark the correct work rather than the incorrect answers to accentuate the positive rather than the negative.

2. Inform the parent(s) of the procedures you will use in assigning homework. Then the parent(s) will know what your expectations are and can be of assistance.

3. Make a sincere effort to "assign" homework that is meaningful and interesting. Be sure it is marked and reviewed in a timely fashion.

4. Keep a record of what types of homework are returned more often than others. If any types of homework are favored, try to utilize this in future assignments.

5. Do not give homework for the sake of homework, but rather when it is necessary. This will give the assignments more meaning to you and the students.

6. Do not to give homework as punishment. This leads to the feeling that all homework is a negative experience.

7. Tell your class convincingly that homework is an earned privilege. The results of this may surprise you!

8. Be sure that you assign for homework only materials that the students fully understand and will be able to do. The parent(s) should not have to teach a skill to a student in order for him to complete the assignment.

9. Phone home to alert parents. Make contracts with students (see Glasser technique).

MANAGEMENT PROBLEM:	*HOMEWORK POLICY AND PROCEDURE*

TEACHER'S CONCERN: What homework policy is fair and at the same time teaches children to assume the responsibility for homework assignments?

WORKABLE OPTIONS:

1. Assign homework on a regular basis so that students are aware that homework is a part of your classroom routine. Try to avoid lengthy weekend assignments.

2. Make assignments brief: 15-20 minutes.

3. Assignments should involve review or reinforcement of skills covered in class that day.

4. Make assignments meaningful. Do not assign busy work for homework.

5. Discuss with your class the value of homework. Allow your students to air their complaints. Do not assume that students understand the reasoning for homework.

6. Use an assignment pad which requires your initials and parents' initials for students who do not return assignments. Make clear to the student that it will be his responsibility to write down the assignments. You initial the assignments as correct. Parents initial the assignments as completed.

7. To help students get assignments home in one piece and also to return work in good condition, encourage the use of plastic folders or book bags. Make folders or homework totes as a class art project. Mark all homework within 24 hours and return to students within that time frame.

8. Use progress charts as a way to encourage daily responsibility of homework. Have meaningful rewards available for high achievers.

MANAGEMENT PROBLEM:	*HYPERACTIVITY—SHIFT IN ATTENTION*

TEACHER'S CONCERN: What can I do for students who frequently shift their attention and/or interests in class?

WORKABLE OPTIONS:

1. Assign the student some type of classroom responsibility that he/she looks forward to doing (e.g., collection of completed work, delivering messages, etc.).

2. Carefully arrange the student's work area to minimize classroom distractions (e.g., study carrels, room partitions, etc.).

3. Plan individual and/or group lessons that foster the development of analytical abilities in your students (e.g., a step-by-step approach in solving everyday problems).

4. Refer the student to a specialist and/or school nurse to check on visual and auditory deficits.

5. Provide your students with firm but fair classroom rules. Make sure you consistently adhere to the rules and enforce the consequences.

6. Use social reinforcers frequently and as soon as possible (e.g., physical nearness or contact, a smile or frown, etc).

7. Prepare a variety of short lessons to maximize student attention and participation (e.g., manipulation exercises of 15 to 20 minutes in duration on elementary level; 5 or 10 minutes on secondary level)

8. Make suggestions to parents about the possibility of using various nutritional diets (e.g., Feingold diet).

9. Regularly incorporate "relaxation" techniques into the daily classroom routine and/or when the students seem to need them.

MANAGEMENT PROBLEM:	*HYPERACTIVITY AND DISTRACTIBILITY*
TEACHER'S CONCERN:	How do I manage the "hyper" student and a student who is limited in the ability to screen out irrelevant stimuli?

WORKABLE OPTIONS:

1. Employ hands-on activities.

2. Eliminate as many environmental distractions as possible.

3. Establish a well-defined work area for the child. This will help to limit outside activities that would detract from his concentration.

4. Use classroom aids such as headphones, tachistoscope, videos, etc. Provide for controlled exposures.

5. Pace activities realistically.

6. Incorporate gross motor skills into activities whenever possible.

7. Use bilateral activities, using hands and eyes, in the lesson.

8. Make an obstacle course and have the students move through it at varying paces.

9. Use a timer. When the timer stops, students may have a short break. Never use a timer to speed up work as it causes tension and frustration rather than increased skill.

10. Have a "time out" period as a reward for a hyperactive child who has spent time doing correct activities.

| MANAGEMENT PROBLEM: | *IMMATURE BEHAVIOR* |

MANAGEMENT PROBLEM: *IMMATURE BEHAVIOR*

TEACHER'S CONCERN: How can the incidence of immature behavior be decreased?

WORKABLE OPTIONS:

1. Evaluate your expectations. Be careful not to pressure or frustrate the children.

2. Ignore undesirable behavior.

3. Establish expected behaviors. Make list a list of relevant behavior that demonstrates meaningful activities, minimal confusion and conflict, positive interaction, and productive activity.

4. Identify problems in the classroom that seem to lead to immature behaviors and try to anticipate them to avoid that behavior.

5. Check to see if your expectations are in line with the student's values.

6. Check for displaced feelings.

7. Check for problems at home.

8. If child exhibiting immature behaviors has been classified, check his file and/or his individualized plan (IEP) for suggestions on how to respond most effectively.

9. Allow children to explain their reasons for use of immature behavior.

10. Consult with colleagues, your school counselor, or a member of the Child Study Team for ideas to cope with this problem.

MANAGEMENT PROBLEM:	*IMPROVING LISTENING SKILLS*

TEACHER'S CONCERN: What do I do with students who seem to be unable to listen and follow directions?

WORKABLE OPTIONS:

1. Check informally for listening. Test students on memory for digits such as 1-7-10 and have students repeat them back to you.

2. Check informally to see if student can hear by dropping a coin behind him and see what happens. Cover your mouth with a piece of paper and determine if he/she can follow what you have said to do.

3. Give the students a series of directions: get the book, shut the door, look up at the light. As students improve, increase the complexity. (This can be played through the game "Simon Says.")

4. Check for sound location. Have students listen for a letter sound, such as "d," and determine whether it comes at the beginning, middle, or end of the word.

5. Have students repeat directions or sentences.

6. Repeat various sequences of words and ask students to write them on a piece of paper in the proper order.

7. Try sequence stories. One student starts a story with a sentence. The next student repeats the first sentence and adds a new one, and so on.

8. Students tell simple jokes or riddles; other students try to remember and repeat them.

9. Play the game "In Grandmother's Attic." The first student starts by saying, "In Grandmother's attic, I found" and gives a word beginning with "a." The next student repeats the "a" word and adds a word beginning with "b." Continue playing through the letter "z."

MANAGEMENT PROBLEM:	*INAPPROPRIATE BEHAVIOR DURING LUNCH AND/OR RECESS*
TEACHER'S CONCERN:	How can behavior during lunch or recess be improved?
WORKABLE OPTIONS:	

1. Establish rules for behavior in lunchroom and recess. Be reasonable with your rules.

2. Deny privileges to students who violate code of expected behavior (see Cantor's Assertive Discipline technique).

3. Make the lunchroom/recess supervisor aware of your behavior code.

4. Role-play situations where foolishness can lead to accidents in the lunchroom or playground.

5. Provide students with a variety of activities to do during recess.

6. Elect table monitors on a weekly basis. This can be done by seating arrangements. For example: In week #1 the child sitting in seat #1 on right side of table will be the monitor; rotate to the next seat each week. This method can be implemented even in a cafeteria where seating is random choice.

7. Reverse the traditional lunch followed by recess routine and have recess first and then lunch. The children have expended a great deal of energy and are more capable of a less active time at lunch. It certainly seems more logical to encourage energetic activity before lunch than after lunch!

8. Set up a large screen TV in the cafeteria and show an appropriate movie (Disney or student choice). The local video store often will provide these free to schools! Choice of film can be a "reward" for good class behavior or class choices picked out of a grab bag.

MANAGEMENT PROBLEM:	*INCOMPLETE CLASS ASSIGNMENTS AND/OR HOMEWORK*

TEACHER'S CONCERN: Some students exhibit an unwillingness to complete class assignments and/or homework for a number of reasons (e.g., absenteeism, inefficient use of student time, unpreparedness, etc.). What can be provided for those students who demonstrate these problems?

WORKABLE OPTIONS:

1. Give the student an assignment at the appropriate level of difficulty. Upon satisfactory completion, let the student "choose" an activity from a class list of reinforcing events (e.g., independent reading, drawing, homework, etc.).

2. Post a chart on the bulletin board stating what materials are to be brought to class each day.

3. Set up a "point" system reinforcing those behaviors that contribute to a student's preparedness. Exchange points earned for special individual and/or group activity (e.g., bring textbooks, notebooks, and supplies to class).

4. Provide the student with a "Term Course Contract." This agreement should carefully delineate what the student is expected to do in order to receive a certain grade and/or course credit. Also, it may be helpful to include "due" dates for long-range assignments, quizzes, major exams, etc.

5. Remind your students, as often as needed, when assignments are due.

6. Use "daily work contracts" for those students who need maximum structure (e.g., "I agree to complete *assignment* by the next *specified time*. Upon completion of my assignment, I will receive an *award*). The teacher and student sign and date the contract.

MANAGEMENT PROBLEM:	*INCONSISTENCY*

TEACHER'S CONCERN: What can I do with students who are inconsistent in routine matters?

WORKABLE OPTIONS:

1. Talk to the student to see if he knows and can say what the routine is.

2. If the student has problems after a considerable time, refer him to the Child Study Team. He may have a perceptual problem or an attention deficit.

3. Be patient. Remind him of the routine. It takes some students more time than others to adjust to a routine.

4. Implement a behavior modification program.

5. Monitor this child frequently. Check to make sure he is doing what he is supposed to be doing.

6. Reinforce this child positively when he is consistent.

7. Involve the parents. See if they notice this at home. Help them establish a reward system for good days (i.e., days on which he followed the routine).

8. Examine the situation you consider "routine." Perhaps it is too complex or you have not allotted a sufficient amount of time for the students to understand, learn, and realize its importance.

9. Examine your reaction to his inconsistency. Is the child being inconsistent to gain your attention? Is so, change your reaction.

10. Does your classroom routine actually reflect good classroom management or are you creating more problems by having such a rigid structure?

MANAGEMENT PROBLEM:	*INDIVIDUAL ATTENTION TO SPECIAL NEEDS STUDENTS*

TEACHER'S CONCERN: A student needs individual attention in order to master a task and/or skill. How can I personalize his instruction?

WORKABLE OPTIONS:

1. Use peer tutors to help the students complete assignments.

2. Provide frequent individual conferences for the student in order to monitor his academic progress.

3. Notify parents about positive growth via Friday notes.

4. Set realistic goals for the student (e.g., modify class assignments when appropriate). Thoroughly review assigned work to ensure proper understanding.

5. Praise the student's achievements frequently in private and public.

6. Organize complex academic tasks into separate units and then place in sequential order for completion.

7. Prepare individual learning packets of work for the student to do. Ask him to return the assignments when completed for evaluation.

8. Use a variety of teaching materials in the classroom (e.g., taped books, videotaped programs, movies, slides, etc.).

9. Provide hands-on projects to help students establish academic concepts (e.g., model building).

10. Use self-correcting materials so that the student may receive immediate feedback (e.g., software).

MANAGEMENT PROBLEM:	*INDIVIDUALIZATION*

TEACHER'S CONCERN: How can I give individual attention in a large classroom?

WORKABLE OPTIONS:

1. Use learning centers based on skills shown to be deficient.

2. Tape record lessons intended for small group work.

3. Make up daily work packets for each child that contain handwriting and other simple review.

4. Try to use work that is self-correcting or has a key that a child can use. (Computer packets are available.)

5. Use student tutors from upper grades for routine work, while you attend to special problems that occur.

6. Implement the use of educational TV.

7. Team-teach when possible to provide more efficient use of time.

8. Use audiovisual materials: language master, Systems 80, tachistoscope.

9. Evaluate grouping arrangements for better utilization of time.

10. Implement individual prescription instruction (IPI) system.

11. Be flexible and willing to change direction when individual needs are evident.

12. Have a grading system so the student can check his work and work at his own pace.

MANAGEMENT PROBLEM:	*INDIVIDUALIZATION: DEPENDENCY*

TEACHER'S CONCERN: What do I do with a student who demands my individual attention for most of the work period and seems to feel he cannot proceed without my personal direction?

WORKABLE OPTIONS:

1. Establish fixed goals for the students and a fixed amount of time to accomplish the goals. Be sure your directions are clear.

2. Institute a "buddy" system. Students will work together to complete work.

3. Place directions on a tape. The student who has difficulty remembering the directions can play the tape back as necessary.

4. Use inviting learning centers for students who have completed their seatwork.

5. Check with the appropriate school personnel to see if this child has a learning problem or lacks processing skills.

6. Make it a policy to send home a note to parents concerning their child's performance for the week. This can be a simple check-off sheet that reflects progress. Encourage parents to reward good progress.

7. Use a timer. When the timer is running, students are to work at their seats. When the timer goes off, the students may take a short break. Never use a timer for the general class to complete work. This may stress students unnecessarily and prevent them from doing their work.

8. Provide access to varied practice sheets that the students may use when they have finished their work.

54

MANAGEMENT PROBLEM:	*INTERRUPTIONS FROM ADMINISTRATION*

TEACHER'S CONCERN:

What can I do about the constant interruptions from the office and pupils sent from other classes with messages?

WORKABLE OPTIONS:

1. First, ask other teachers if they feel the same way concerning classroom interruptions. This will ensure that there is an accurate focus on the effect of this problem.

2. At the next faculty or liaison meeting, ask that the problem be discussed and that possible solutions be offered and analyzed for feasibility.

3. If, for some reason, you are hesitant to confront the administration or fellow teachers with this concern, submit thoughts, feelings, and possible solutions in written form to the administration for suggestions and clarification.

4. When a child interrupts your class with a note, read it and then tell the student to tell the 'sender" that you will respond to the message at lunch or another time (unless the answer is "yes" or "no").

5. Ask the principal to inform teachers in the special areas to adhere to their predetermined schedules so that the classroom teachers can better plan their day and not be interrupted at an unexpected time.

6. When testing, place a sign on your door that states, "PLEASE DO NOT DISTURB—TESTING."

7. Request that the office make announcements on the public address system only at the same scheduled times of the day (e.g., morning announcements, closing-of-school announcements).

8. Prepare a plan that will facilitate communication without interruption.

MANAGEMENT PROBLEM:	*INTERRUPTIONS DURING GROUP WORK*
TEACHER'S CONCERN:	How can I cope with children who interrupt me during group work with legitimate questions regarding their individual assigned task?

WORKABLE OPTIONS:

1. Appoint group captains. Use more conscientious students for this job. They can help to answer questions for you.

2. Use a stop/go sign to indicate when you are available for questioning. These can be purchased at any teacher supply store.

3. Give students some free time to seek your attention between sessions of group work. Take a snack break.

4. Discuss with your class reasons for the need for uninterrupted group sessions.

5. Reward the class for periods of uninterrupted work.

6. Give students guidance on how to skip areas of uncertainty and move on to work that they know so they do not spend all of their time waiting for the helper or for the break time to talk to you.

7. Try to give equal time to each group so that the students at their seats are not expected to work for unrealistic extended periods. The younger the class, the shorter the period should be.

8. Be sure that the assignments given to each group are clear and precise so that the participants will not have as many questions.

9. Provide easy access in your classroom to supplementary resource materials dealing with the topics of the group assignment. Encourage their use by having students work independently and in groups.

MANAGEMENT PROBLEM:	*LACK OF COMMONSENSE BEHAVIOR*

TEACHER'S CONCERN: What can I do to improve commonsense knowledge of my students?

WORKABLE OPTIONS:

1. Have a conference with the student to help give examples of how using common sense is important in everyday classroom routine, as well as in life in general.

2. Make sure the student thinks carefully before he says or writes something in class.

3. Talk to the parents about the problem. They can help the child develop commonsense skills at home.

4. Develop a unit within the class. Have a group identify "commonsense" knowledge. Follow up with classification of how common sense is used in everyday activity.

5. Discuss how using common sense is a way to be safe (e.g., provide examples of how common sense on the playground keeps a child from getting hurt).

6. Role-play activities that demonstrate use of commonsense reactions to everyday school situations.

7. Have students identify how classroom rules reflect common sense.

8. Try to help students realize that common sense is actually a logical reaction to a situation. Discuss what makes something logical (safe, polite, reasonable, etc.).

| MANAGEMENT PROBLEM: | *LACK OF DISCIPLINE AT HOME: Part 1* |

TEACHER'S CONCERN: How can I deal with children whose parents are not supportive of school-recommended disciplinary steps at home that spill over into school behavior?

WORKABLE OPTIONS:

1. Be aware of the fact that each home has its own management system and there will be times when the program of the school may conflict with the value system and procedures of the home. The school can try to make changes but will not always succeed. Teachers have an obligation to try and should understand that lack of success is not necessarily the same as failure.

2. Implement a behavior modification program (see Krumboltz, Skinner, Thomas) to be used with students needing structured discipline.

3. Bring the child's parent(s) into the problem in a positive manner. Ask their advice and share their concerns. Invite them in for conferences and be thoroughly prepared with anecdotal notes concerning the child's behavior. Involve the principal, Child Study Team, and/or department heads if necessary to support your concern.

4. Use the technique of sending home daily behavior reports to parents who have agreed to cooperate. Always begin these reports on a positive note. This personalized communication demonstrates to the parents that you are willing to go "that extra mile" for their child even though you have many children in your class.

5. Develop a positive relationship with the home by contacting parents to provide information of good behavior rather than just negative reports. Explain how productive it is to "catch the student doing something good" to encourage and identify clearly positive behavior.

MANAGEMENT PROBLEM:	*LACK OF DISCIPLINE AT HOME: Part 2*
TEACHER'S CONCERN:	What can I do to reach parents of undisciplined students?

WORKABLE OPTIONS:

1. If you deny the student privileges in school as the result of behavior, be sure that it relates directly to the rule violated. Discipline must he a learning experience. (See Cantor's Assertive Discipline program.) Give parents information on the discipline program you are using so they understand the process and procedures.

2. Play the game "What is ahead for me?" Discuss the consequences of the student's behavior. List future happenings that might occur if he improves. List items that may occur if he continues to misbehave. Share this with the child's parents.

3. Constantly reexamine your relationship with the child and parent. Are you being overly sensitive? Are you "picking on" one child? Have you stigmatized this child because of the reputation of his siblings?

4. Review the child's cumulative folder to see if there is any indication that his behavior is characteristic throughout his school experience.

5. Keep anecdotal records that note when behavior occurs. Share with the parent(s) whether he works better in the morning than in the afternoon or what seems to trigger his negative behavior in class. Ask if anything at home stimulates this behavior (e.g., lack of sleep, no breakfast, etc.).

| MANAGEMENT PROBLEM: | *LACK OF INTEREST IN ACADEMICS* |

TEACHER'S CONCERN: How can I deal with a student who places emphasis on sports rather than academics?

WORKABLE OPTIONS:

1. Ask members of the honor society to speak to your class. Have them stress the prestige and value of learning.

2. Call the parents. Explain that such an attitude will hinder progress. Stress the need for them to work with you as a team to change this attitude.

3. Obtain books for the student to read that give biographical data on outstanding athletes who were successful academically in college and became doctors, lawyers, etc.).

4. Reward high academic achievers through contests and competition in classroom work.

5. Be aware that teachers must deal with parents' value systems and be accepting of these values.

6. Us the game "Goalpost" as an incentive. Set up a goalpost on the bulletin board. Each day set a goal for each child. As he completes goals set, he crosses over the goalpost. If goals aren't completed, discuss reasons that prevented success.

7. Work with the teachers involved in sport activities to stimulate better student performance in academics. Encourage them to show how they need to know math, science, art, etc., in order to follow a play or participate in a sports activity (e.g., scores and running distances to mathematics, past records in sports to history).

8. Never use the threat of denial. "If you don't do well you will not be able to participate in the game." It doesn't work.

MANAGEMENT PROBLEM:	*LACK OF MOTIVATION: Part 1*

TEACHER'S CONCERN: What do I do with students who lack motivation, have a very negative attitude toward school, and come to class unprepared?

WORKABLE OPTIONS:

1. Do everything possible to make sure the physical condition of the student has been met. Has he eaten breakfast, had enough rest, can he see the board clearly, hear clearly, etc.?

2. Make your classroom interesting and stimulating to the students. Make your lessons inviting and challenging so students want to find out what will come next!

3. Show your students that you take an interest in them, that you like them, and that they belong in your classroom.

4. Make your lesson an experience that allows the student to gain self-esteem because he is successful and a vital member of the class.

5. Establish challenging but attainable goals.

6. Take advantage of the student's interest and formulate some lessons around them.

7. When developing practice worksheets, use the students' names and something you know about them to teach a concept (e.g., "Susan expressed her enjoyment regarding her trip to Walt Disney World" when identifying parts of speech).

8. Send home weekly reports to parents. Encourage parents to reward for high motivation.

9. Use the concept of working together (such as cooperative learning groups) to encourage each other.

10. Have students chart their behavior for a week.

MANAGEMENT PROBLEM:	*LACK OF MOTIVATION: Part 2*

TEACHER'S CONCERN: What methods can I use to motivate my students' interest in learning?

WORKABLE OPTIONS:

1. Use incentives in the classroom, such as prizes, stars, and rewards for completing assignments on time, to reinforce motivation toward accomplishment.

2. Get to know each child as an individual to gain insight into his strengths and interests.

3. Have monthly conferences with students discussing work habits, motivation, behavior, etc.

4. Have real purpose in the schoolwork you assign so it relates to their needs.

5. Assist the student in setting realistic goals.

6. Don't always point out errors on a student's work, but show how improvement can be made on the finished product.

7. Provide editing time when you work one-on-one with students in perfecting their creative work.

8. Show enthusiasm while you teach because the teacher is the key to motivation in the classroom.

9. Develop special projects for the child whose interests have not yet been tapped by the school routine.

10. Create special recognition through "student of the month" or "star for the day." See "Ticket Program" in Section II. pp. 108-111.

MANAGEMENT PROBLEM:	*LACK OF RESPECT*

TEACHER'S CONCERN: What do I do with students who show a lack of respect for adults, peers, their belongings, and property of others?

WORKABLE OPTIONS:

1. The teacher should practice the 3 *R*'s: respect, responsibility, and reciprocity.

2. Role-play situations where there is lack of respect. Example: Someone fails a test and others make fun of that person. Follow with group analysis and discuss the situation and alternative actions.

3. Clearly state the reasons for respecting other people's property. Publicly acknowledge those who show respect so peers can model their behavior.

4. Show videos dealing with respect and then discuss them. See Guidance Associates materials. Obtain materials from your county audio library.

5. Don't make unrealistic requests, dictate rules without explanations, or give ultimatums that will give students a boundary that they might be tempted to break because they feel it is unreasonable.

6. Listen to each student. Never automatically assume you know what the student is going to say.

7. Show that even though you are in charge of the class, you respect the student and expect respect in return.

8. Never give idle unrealistic threats (e.g., "How many times have I told you to sit down? I am going to have to take away your recess time for the semester unless you behave.")!

MANAGEMENT PROBLEM:	*LACK OF SELF-ESTEEM IN STUDENT REQUIRED TO RECEIVE OUTSIDE CLASSROOM AID*

TEACHER'S CONCERN:

How can I make students feel better about themselves and their self-worth and still have them participate in outside instructional services?

WORKABLE OPTIONS:

1. Let the student know that the additional help is there to improve his academic achievement and is not a punishment. Tell him there are many students who receive this aid and who have potential and are special.

2. Encourage the student on his progress and give abundant praise.

3. Reward the student appropriately for his success in the special instructional program.

4. Provide many opportunities for the student to succeed while he is participating in regular class activities so that he feels he belongs.

5. Have a conference with the parent(s) so they will support and encourage the student at home to improve the skills for which he is receiving extra help.

6. Use the services of the school guidance counselor if you feel lack of self-esteem is a major concern.

7. Develop a program for teachers and students explaining the merits of out-of-class special instruction to give it a positive place in the school curriculum.

8. Set up a bulletin board displaying good work and include the work done well by students attending special instructional classes. This should make him confident and comfortable about his place in his regular class.

MANAGEMENT	
PROBLEM:	*LEARNING CENTERS*

**TEACHER'S
CONCERN:** I would like to use learning centers in the classroom. Where can I get information in this area?

**WORKABLE
OPTIONS:**

1. First, observe a teacher who has successfully implemented learning centers in the classroom. This information and permission can be obtained from the administration or the teacher.

2. Plan a visit to a learning center in your state. You can find out where they are by contacting your district and/or state educational offices. In New Jersey there are Educational Improvement Centers (EIC) located at colleges and special buildings. The State Department of Education in Trenton can provide you with specific locations. These centers have workshops, literature, and complete learning center materials that can be borrowed for classroom use.

3. There are many books available at your local library that provide details on the development and use of learning centers. They are excellent sources for ideas and procedures that have worked successfully in the classroom.

4. Complete materials can be purchased at teacher supply stores to make up an interest center. Once you get the idea, it is easy to develop your own models.

5. Build an interest center reflecting a curriculum area as a classroom project.

6. If space is available, designate a room in the school where teachers can display and share learning centers that they have purchased or made. This would be similar to a "Science Fair" but would actually be a "Learning Center Fair" that could be on display for parents as well. Get permission from your administrator to initiate this idea.

MANAGEMENT PROBLEM:	*LISTENING*
TEACHER'S CONCERN:	What do I do with students who will not listen?

WORKABLE OPTIONS:

1. Have the student's hearing tested.

2. Have the student's auditory perception tested by the school's learning consultant or psychologist.

3. If results from options 1 and 2 are both negative, assume that the student does not choose to listen or may have an attention deficit.

4. Is the student daydreaming or preoccupied with something else? If so, repeat what you have asked him.

5. Discuss with the student his listening problem. See what is on his mind.

6. If there is no open relationship between you and the student, find another person with whom he can relate (e.g., the school counselor, another teacher, or one of his friends).

7. Do not consistently repeat yourself. Attach a consequence if your directions are not followed after saying it once. Be sure to speak clearly and be consistent in enforcing your listening rules.

8. Discuss your expectations and consequences in the beginning of the school year. Speak clearly and precisely.

9. Try not to give too many directions at the same time. Some students cannot retain a long sequence of directions.

10. Be sensitive and listen to the students so that they will model your behavior.

MANAGEMENT	
PROBLEM:	*LISTENING SKILLS DEVELOPMENT*

TEACHER'S CONCERN: Is there any way to improve listening skills in the classroom?

WORKABLE OPTIONS:

1. Contact the reading specialist in your district. This person is a valuable resource for providing or sharing techniques and materials to develop students' listening skills.

2. Especially in the upper grades, explain to the students that they will be evaluated by a test after any group discussion. This will motivate the students to use and develop listening skills.

3. In your closure after each lesson, be sure you review with your students what they have learned so they will see the need for listening attentively.

4. Be sure that you and the students know what "listening skills" mean, and that the students are able to understand the important basic facts of a lesson.

5. Attend professional workshops that provide information on developing listening skills in your classroom.

6. In the lower grades, ask the students to write down in list form as many facts or ideas they can remember after a class discussion.

7. Offer listening skill awards for students who demonstrate progress in this area. Recognize publicly when a student shows he has listened and interpreted a concept correctly and thoughtfully during a class activity or discussion.

| MANAGEMENT PROBLEM: | *LOW FRUSTRATION TOLERANCE* |

MANAGEMENT PROBLEM: *LOW FRUSTRATION TOLERANCE*

TEACHER'S CONCERN: How can we successfully challenge our students but still remain within the limits of their frustration range?

WORKABLE OPTIONS:

1. Provide many different opportunities for students to cope with gradual doses of mild frustration and increased difficulty.

2. Plan activities that ensure more success than failure for students (e.g., independent projects of their own choosing).

3. Respond to the student's frustration by reducing or changing performance demands (e.g., reinforce partially correct responses, shorten assignments, etc.)

4. Organize complex tasks into separate parts. Present the material in a logical, sequential order for completion.

5. Make every effort to give positive feedback to students who have successfully completed their assignments.

6. Personalize academic instruction for students who need additional help in alleviating some of their frustrations.

7. Try to anticipate when the student will become frustrated, and then change the activity accordingly.

8. Allow the student to work at his own pace.

9. Help the student to develop a positive self image.

10. If the problem persists, refer the student to the appropriate school personnel.

MANAGEMENT PROBLEM:	*LYING TO AUTHORITY FIGURES*

TEACHER'S CONCERN: When confronted with students who are obviously lying, what are some viable options for handling the situation?

WORKABLE OPTIONS:

1. Realize that what is dishonest for mature adults may not be for the student's peers. Plan activities that improve the student's perception of honesty and how to implement it in everyday situations.

2. Provide consistent discipline and positive but firm classroom rules. Keep your promises to students.

3. Give opportunities for students to express their negative feelings (e.g., private conferences, class discussions, written assignments, etc., as general class activities).

4. Use activities that will build feelings of mutual respect with peers and/or adults (e.g., group projects involving work in the community).

5. Be calm and rational when you know a student is not telling the truth by not making it the center of the classroom discussion. **Give positive attention** when the student displays courage to be honest ("You impressed me when you acknowledged that you were involved in that incident").

6. If a student is being defensive when lying, it may be result of years of punitive discipline. Instead of punishing him severely, provide positive discipline techniques that will not force more responsibility than he can handle (e.g., write a short theme on the topic "Positive effects of admitting when you are wrong").

7. Praise students who obviously lie to impress their peers whenever they are being honest.

| MANAGEMENT PROBLEM: | *MISUSE OF TEACHERS' OR AIDES' TIME* |

| TEACHER'S CONCERN: | What do I do when students constantly come up to me for help? |

WORKABLE OPTIONS:

1. Make a tape recording with animal sounds. Assign each group of five students an animal sound. When they hear their sound, they can come up to the teacher's desk for questions, to tell a story, etc.

2. On a daily basis, provide a short period of time when students sit in a circle and discuss questions, stories, or problems. Encourage students to save discussion throughout the day for this circle time.

3. Make a schedule that provides a short time for each student to discuss concerns with the teacher.

4. Discourage students from coming up to the teacher's desk at inappropriate times.

5. Provide an "instant gratification" sheet where a student may write down briefly his immediate need. The teacher can scan this quickly and respond to those who need immediate attention between groups or at convenient times.

6. Provide classroom helpers to respond to questions about the independent work students are doing. (See *Attention-Seeking Well-Behaved Student*, p. 12.)

7. Provide clearly-stated rules so the students do not need to ask the teacher for everything (e.g., a pass for the bathroom; availability of paper, pencils, extra worksheets; etc., which can be used by the students without asking the teacher).

MANAGEMENT	
PROBLEM:	*MOTIVATION TO COMPLETE ASSIGNMENTS*

**TEACHER'S
CONCERN:** How can students with ability be motivated to complete assignments even though they say "I can't"?

**WORKABLE
OPTIONS:**

1. Check to see if there are any physical reasons for the student's inability to handle independent work. The school nurse or family doctor can look for visual, auditory, perceptual problems, low energy level, or lack of ability to concentrate.

2. Plan activities that revolve around student interest.

3. Insure success in the independent work given the students. It should be neither too difficult nor too easy to complete.

4. Allow children to express their likes and dislikes in regards to independent work. Make your standards known so they are fully aware of what you consider satisfactory work.

5. Provide space for the students to establish interest centers; encourage those students who lack motivation to develop centers illustrating their hobbies and talents.

6. Provide a classroom that is attractive and stimulating with resource materials easily accessible. Make the experience successful.

7. Reward the students who show progress so that every student in the room has an opportunity to be rewarded. Incorporate topics of interest to the students.

8. Establish goals with each child and reinforce with frequent review and personal interaction.

9. Evaluate (mark) children's work as quickly as possible to eliminate frustration and prevent reinforcement of erroneous concepts.

MANAGEMENT PROBLEM:	*NAME CALLING, SOMETIMES RACIAL*
TEACHER'S CONCERN:	What do I do with students who call other students names, sometimes with racial overtones?
WORKABLE OPTIONS:	

1. Show videos depicting various cultures and discuss variations in each. Emphasize that being different is not bad.

2. Role-play name-calling situations and have a discussion afterward.

3. Assign groups of students to a different culture. Using cooperative learning groups, have students develop a group skit to be presented at a "Multicultural Fair" with each group showing their culture's dress, food, language, etc.

4. Establish rules concerning name calling, coupled with strict consequences for disobeying these rules.

5. Reward students for not responding aggressively to other students calling them names.

6. Provide activities that illustrate the unfairness of prejudice and name calling, such as: (a) having only blue-eyed students participate in a favorite activity, (b) allowing only boys to get a drink, etc. This shows the unfairness of bias. Let children explore the multitude of ways they can be "classified" and the unfairness of this. Show the film *Blue Eyes, Brown Eyes*.

7. Ask the students to report on real-life situations different from their own. (What would it be like to live on the streets? What would be different if you lived in Alaska?) Develop presentations for the class.

MANAGEMENT PROBLEM:	*NEGATIVE RESPONSE TO REQUESTS AND RULES*

TEACHER'S CONCERN: When confronted with students who are negative about rational requests and/or rules, what are some of my possible options?

WORKABLE OPTIONS:

1. Try to use these guidelines when establishing classroom rules:

   a) Involve your class in making up the rules.
   b) State the rules positively.
   c) Rules should be brief and to the point.
   d) Review rules periodically with the class.

2. Arrange private conferences with students to discuss the problem in depth.

3. Ask the student(s) to write down the disturbing behavior in a class logbook. Have him write some appropriate ways of responding to negativity.

4. Provide choices for students to minimize negative reactions (e.g., "Would you rather stay an extra ten minutes and finish the exercise before lunch, or go to lunch now and finish it when you come back?").

5. Try to produce frequent positive interaction in the class (e.g., praise, group projects, discussions, etc.).

6. Make sure students clearly understand what is expected from them. (In some cases, it's the student's confusion that causes oppositional behavior.)

7. Handle difficult students individually outside the classroom so that there is less of a chance of others getting involved.

8. Contact parents, the principal, and/or counselor to discuss the student's inappropriate behavior.

MANAGEMENT PROBLEM:	*NERVOUS HABITS IN CLASSROOM*

TEACHER'S CONCERN:

What do I do with a student who has a habit of chewing on erasers, crayons, and pencils?

WORKABLE OPTIONS:

1. Determine if too much pressure is being placed on the student, causing him to develop a nervous habit.

2. Have a parent conference to find out if there are any stress situations taking place at home.

3. Have a student conference to discuss concerns and the fact that the habit annoys others.

4. Provide rewards for the student who conforms to the rules and shows improvement in controlling this behavior.

5. If pencils or crayons are too tempting for the student, collect them after activities are completed.

6. Establish a "Behavior Modification" program (Skinner) to wean the student away from these habits.

7. Seek the professional expertise of the school psychologist.

MANAGEMENT PROBLEM:	*NOISY WORK HABITS*

TEACHER'S CONCERN: What do I do with a few students who constantly call out or talk loudly while other students are working quietly? How can I efficiently control the noise level of the classroom?

WORKABLE OPTIONS:

1. Provide frequent breaks and a change of pace.

2. Reward students for not calling out in class.

3. Provide learning centers that students may go to after completing their work.

4. Place the "constant talker" away from other students or provide him with a study carrel to limit distractions.

5. Maintain a progress chart on the bulletin board recording the positive independent work of students.

6. For questions, have students hold up a sign with a question mark on it that you can see and respond to.

7. Provide individual task cards for students to do when their assignment is completed.

8. Play soft music as a reward when students are working in non-academic areas and have kept the class noise level down.

9. Combine desirable activities with less desirable activities. If an activity holds the children's interest, less talking will take place.

10. Clarify reasons for the benefits of a quiet work time.

11. Establish clear rules during seatwork and enforce them consistently.

| MANAGEMENT PROBLEM: | *NOT DRESSED FOR GYM* |

**MANAGEMENT
PROBLEM:** *NOT DRESSED FOR GYM*

**TEACHER'S
CONCERN:** What can I do if a student does not attend detention when he does not dress for gym, which is a school rule?

**WORKABLE
OPTIONS:**

1. Have another student walk with him to the detention room to make sure he gets there.

2. Take away certain privileges if the student cuts detention.

3. Have a conference with the parents of the student to explain that the student is not dressing for gym and refuses to go to detention.

4. Report the problem to the principal and see if he can help out.

5. Give the student extra work if he is not prepared for gym.

6. Discuss the problem with the student in private to see what his reasons are for not being prepared.

7. Talk to the gym teacher to see if he has some insight into the problem.

8. If it is an economic problem (child cannot afford gym outfit), see the school nurse about contacting a local service agency that will provide for the student (community centers, service agencies, etc.).

9. Talk calmly and privately to the student to determine if his reluctance to participate in gym is due to another significant reason (embarrassment about physical appearance, lack of coordination and skill, etc.).

MANAGEMENT PROBLEM:	*OFF-TASK BEHAVIOR*

TEACHER'S CONCERN: What do I do with students who are not doing what they are supposed to do? These students will talk and play, waste time, move about the room, etc., rather than work on class assignments.

WORKABLE OPTIONS:

1. Discuss expectations with the class at the beginning of the year.

2. Discuss expectations in private with students who are having difficulty keeping on task.

3. Write the task on the board. If daily seatwork assignments are given, write this in the same location daily so students get into the habit of looking for their assignments.

4. Hold each student responsible for the assignment. Check work individually on a daily basis. The student will be more likely to do it if he knows you will definitely check to see if it's done.

5. Attach consequences to uncompleted tasks.

6. Attach a consequence for being off-task (talking, walking around, playing).

7. Examine the cause. Is the task too easy? Is it too difficult? Are you inconsistent in enforcing the consequences? Is the consequence not severe enough to discourage this behavior?

8. Employ a firm behavior modification program.

9. Contact the parents. Try an at-home reward system. Send home daily reports concerning the student's behavior.

10. Have the child checked for a potential hearing problem or a health problem that makes it difficult for him to sit quietly for extended periods.

MANAGEMENT PROBLEM:	*PRESTIGE: EQUAL VALUE TO ALL SUBJECTS, INCLUDING ART*
TEACHER'S CONCERN:	Other subject area teachers indicate that art is not as important as other subjects, and this attitude is transferred to the students. How can I make teachers and students understand the importance of art as part of the school curriculum?

WORKABLE OPTIONS:

1. Explain to the students the importance of art and the people who have contributed in the history of art.

2. Ask the principal if you can give a presentation to faculty regarding the role art plays in teaching academic subjects.

3. Have art lessons that are appropriate for your students' needs, as well as complementary to the academic work in which they are currently involved. Encourage input from their teachers.

4. Work with the principal in scheduling your classes so they do not frustrate other staff members.

5. Bring in video, films, and projects; suggest field trips to museums; display your students' art throughout the school to demonstrate the role of art in everyday experiences.

6. Help the classroom teachers with their bulletin board displays. You will endear yourself to them with this offer alone!

7. Establish the tradition of a yearly art festival to display the outstanding work of students. If this is not possible, plan it in conjunction with the yearly open house or teacher conference weeks.

| MANAGEMENT PROBLEM: | *PAPERWORK* |

**MANAGEMENT
PROBLEM:**   *PAPERWORK*

**TEACHER'S
CONCERN:**   How do I deal more effectively with paperwork?

**WORKABLE
OPTIONS:**

1. When developing assignments and tests, keep in mind the evaluation process. How difficult will they be to grade?

2. Train capable students to do some of the paperwork. They could save you a considerable amount of time by placing papers in alphabetical order, filing, separating different materials, and simple grading using a grading template.

3. If, in your opinion, an unnecessary amount of paperwork is coming from the office, request a liaison meeting to evaluate and perhaps reduce or combine the forms requested.

4. Ask the administration to schedule a workshop where fellow teachers share their techniques of dealing with paperwork.

5. Develop some basic forms you can use to keep records of student progress.

6. Have students keep a work folder that can be used to store their work and provide a good comparative analysis of their progress throughout the year, as well as points of information for parent-teacher conferences.

7. Be sure that your assignments are not just busy work that you must grade. Remember, any and all papers and work assigned to the students must be graded within a reasonable time or the students will feel it was of no value to complete.

8. In simple drill situations, students can exchange papers and grade each other's work as they determine the correct responses. This has double value: it provides review and gives instant response.

MANAGEMENT
PROBLEM:	*PARENTAL INVOLVEMENT WITH THEIR CHILDREN*

TEACHER'S
CONCERN: How do I get the parents involved in their children's welfare in the classroom environment?

WORKABLE
OPTIONS:

1. Periodically telephone the parents and tell them about the child's successful progress in all areas; conclude with areas that they are working on.

2. Have the parents use reinforcement procedures at home and give some suggestions on how this is done at your first "Open House."

3. Send out a letter to all your students before the school year welcoming them to your class and presenting a brief synopsis of the major areas of learning that you plan for that school year.

4. Communicate with the parents on a regular basis other than the report card. Monthly updates are helpful. Personalize these conversations if there is a problem or something especially productive has happened with their child in class.

5. Make the parents feel welcome and free to visit your classroom at any time.

6. Read and get ideas from many professional books and journals regarding parent-teacher involvement.

7. Visit the child's home if there is extended absence, or if you have never met the parent, to show that you are willing to provide the best possible learning environment for each child in your class.

MANAGEMENT PROBLEM:	*PARENT SUPPORT PROCEDURES*

TEACHER'S CONCERN: Is it possible to increase parental support for the classroom teacher?

WORKABLE OPTIONS:

1. Publish a monthly newspaper, co-authored by the teacher and the students, to inform the parents of what is occurring in the classroom and to share the exceptional and creative work of the students. Make every effort to see that the end of the school year includes all students.

2. On PTA meeting evenings, open your classroom one-half hour before the announced starting time and encourage parents to attend so they can see your classroom and talk to you. This is especially helpful for parents who have more than one student in the same school. Give students of non-involved parents special attention.

3. At the beginning of the school year, inform the parent(s) what you plan to accomplish in the coming months. Be absolutely clear in stating their role and responsibility. Emphasize that parental involvement is vital in fulfilling goals.

4. Attend workshops or seminars that give you ideas on how to improve parent and teacher interaction.

5. Ask the administration to establish parental involvement as a district goal and state that clearly in the calendar distributed at the beginning of the school year.

6. Send a questionnaire to the parents asking for their ideas on how to increase parental involvement and support in the classroom.

7. Provide parenting workshops for parents.

8. Establish a Community Advisory Board that will meet monthly to review school policy decisions.

MANAGEMENT PROBLEM:	*PLANNING AND INNOVATION*

TEACHER'S CONCERN:

How can I be innovative and follow strict planning at the same time? When using a technique new to me and/or my students, it is difficult to estimate the length of the lesson or the follow-up that will be necessary. Yet, if observed, I am expected to be doing exactly what the lesson plan states.

WORKABLE OPTIONS:

1. Block out a section in the weekly lesson plan that will be used to try new teaching techniques or to implement new ideas. Have an explanation written into the plans stating that the factors, such as time, associated with this lesson may not be accurate or known because of the nature of the lesson.

2. Keep the administrator well-informed when you are trying a new approach or technique. This way, he will have a better understanding of the lesson if you happen to be observed. In fact, he most certainly will be supportive of your "adventure" into new horizons and may make a special effort to observe your new idea and give positive and helpful feedback!

3. When trying a new technique have the principal, if practical, be involved as a resource for ideas and recommendations. When changes are made within the lesson plan, cooperation with the principal will more likely occur.

4. Explain orally or in written form that if an increase in professional growth is expected from the teaching staff, there must be more flexibility in the district's policy toward "lesson planning."

5. Share your concerns and ideas with another teacher who is working on the same topic or unit. Find out how he has fared, what has been a successful timeframe, or what procedures have worked most productively.

MANAGEMENT PROBLEM:	*PLAYGROUND INTERACTION*

TEACHER'S CONCERN: What do I do with the student who keeps other students in turmoil on the playground because he keeps making them choose sides, won't play with some of them, has a complaint about all decisions being made, is overly aggressive, etc.?

WORKABLE OPTIONS:

1. Establish rules for expected behavior during playground periods.

2. Establish with the person in charge of playground what behavior you expect from your students during recess.

3. Follow through with corrective behavior on the playground.

4. Praise students for good reports of behavior on the playground.

5. Isolate students for misconduct (e.g., sit five minutes on the curb to settle down).

6. Show a film on safety on the playground and discuss safety rules with your class.

7. Teach students games that can be played on the playground.

8. Indicate areas for specific play activities (e.g., jump rope, basketball boundaries, baseball boundaries, racing games, etc.) so there is no overlapping or conflict.

9. Introduce the "Assertive Discipline" (Cantor) and Glasser's "Reality Therapy" program to be used for playground management.

10. Select a weekly "playground monitor" from your class to help manage appropriate behavior of your students as a model for others.

| MANAGEMENT PROBLEM: | *POOR ADJUSTMENT TO CHANGE IN ENVIRONMENT* |

**MANAGEMENT
PROBLEM:**   *POOR ADJUSTMENT TO CHANGE IN ENVIRONMENT*

**TEACHER'S
CONCERN:**   Some students have difficulty coping with new and/or
                    unfamiliar tasks or situations, and may even attempt to avoid
                    them. How can I improve students' flexibility in new
                    situations?

**WORKABLE
OPTIONS:**

1. Praise students frequently when they make the slightest improvement toward change (e.g., "Bob, I see you're beginning your assignment. Keep up the good work!").

2. Reinforce students with a familiar and enjoyable special activity when they make adjustments in their understanding of a new concept, rule, and/or attitude.

3. Introduce new routines and/or instructional materials to the class via small groups or individually in order to minimize student anxiety.

4. Try to involve the students when making decisions about changes in classroom routines, so that they feel comfortable about the new procedures.

5. Explain change to any students who have been absent during the original introduction of the new process or procedure.

6. Use private conferences to make a student aware of the need to be flexible.

7. Encourage students to slowly develop risk-taking skills so they may confront daily problems with new strategies.

8. Provide many opportunities for students to learn how to cope with their physical and social environment (e.g., role playing).

MANAGEMENT PROBLEM:	*POOR ATTITUDE IN AND TOWARD SCHOOL*

TEACHER'S CONCERN: What can I do to improve a student's attitude in school?

WORKABLE OPTIONS:

1. Be enthused about the subject you are teaching and sensitive to the needs of your students so they will develop favorable attitudes toward you and the subject.

2. Punishing or ridiculing student responses will develop negative attitudes toward you and the subjects being taught. Sarcasm is a negative and non-productive trait; avoid that form of ridicule no matter how frustrating a student may be to you.

3. Have a group discussion to promote insight into the development of positive attitudes.

4. Use role playing to analyze productive and nonproductive attitudes.

5. Rather than reject a student's response completely, find something positive to identify and move on from there. Rejection leads to hopelessness and feelings of failure.

6. Give students the opportunity to experience satisfaction with their acceptable attitudes toward the subject discussed or behavior required so that they will be reinforced in a positive way.

7. Provide motivation in your classroom so children will identify and be inspired to form sound values.

8. Provide a pleasant atmosphere in the classroom. Make demands realistic and the curriculum more suitable to meet the needs of the students.

| MANAGEMENT PROBLEM: | *POOR OR NONEXISTENT WORK HABITS* |

MANAGEMENT PROBLEM: *POOR OR NONEXISTENT WORK HABITS*

TEACHER'S CONCERN: What do I do with students who do not complete their assigned work in class or at home?

WORKABLE OPTIONS:

1. Have a class discussion on the importance of work in the community and of being a responsible citizen.

2. Have students set up career goals.

3. Relate success in schoolwork to their success in their future vocations.

4. Keep a constant check on seatwork by moving around the classroom and glancing at students' progress.

5. Establish an agreement with the parents. Send home notes containing the student's work for that day or call them during the day letting them know what the work is. If the work is still not done, obtain permission for after-school detention to complete the work.

6. Attach clear consequences to incomplete work (e.g., an additional assignment, being placed in another classroom to complete work, withholding a special project, etc.).

7. Institute a reward system to increase productivity. The reward must be meaningful—something the student wants (e.g., a homework excuse pass, permission to use an interest center or internet, etc.).

8. Confer with parents and help them establish a reward system for completing work and responsibilities around the house. Send home notes concerning completed work to be rewarded.

9. Mention the student to the school social worker. Perhaps there is something happening at home that prevents him from doing homework.

MANAGEMENT PROBLEM:	*PRIDE IN ONE'S WORK*

TEACHER'S CONCERN:	I would like to see the students take more pride in their work. What can I do?

WORKABLE OPTIONS:

1. Be sure that you, as an educator, set an example for the students to follow. Be a person who takes pride in his work (e.g., all work papers and letters sent home are neat and accurate, you are well prepared for each lesson, etc.).

2. Occasionally ask the students to evaluate their own work using the same grading system you use. This procedure will enable the children to reflect and decide upon the level and quality of their performance in school. Require that they give rationales for their conclusions (e.g., why they deserve each grade).

3. Throughout the school year, have group discussions with the class about people in the past and present who have achieved significant accomplishments and made noteworthy contributions to society. Have them explore how these people demonstrated pride in their work.

4. Simply ask the student when submitting work if he is proud of his work. If they say no, take time to discuss the reason why. Grade papers on four qualities basic to work well done: complete, correct, concise, and comprehensive.

5. Have a bulletin board set aside for students to place any schoolwork that they are proud to display for their parents to see at "Open House."

6. Show honest joy and enthusiasm for a well-done project or assignment.

7. Verbally recognize all students, especially those never before acknowledged for work well done, so they too can enjoy the feeling of success in front of their peers.

MANAGEMENT PROBLEM:	*PUTTING PROPER IDENTIFICATION ON PAPERS*

TEACHER'S CONCERN: How can I teach children to remember to put the correct identification on papers before turning them in?

WORKABLE OPTIONS:

1. Discuss with the class the importance of putting names on papers.

2. Remind children before actual work begins to place identification on papers.

3. Provide work clues such as: Name: _____ on worksheets.

4. Provide rewards for children who properly label work. Use stars, stickers, stamps, comments, etc.

5. Verbally praise children who correctly identify papers.

6. Attach an undesirable task as a consequence of forgetting to put names on work.

7. Make a personal reminder mobile. Use thick yarn and 3×5 cards. List in sequence the tasks needed to successfully complete a written task. Hang the cards on each child's desk as a guide.

8. Make a pride line using the student's name. List items that the child is proud of (e.g., Sue Jones—proud of her math score). This will help the child use his/her name for positive identification.

9. Never rip up or deface a paper because the name was forgotten. This is an inappropriately severe punishment.

10. Choose a group captain for classroom chores. The captain checks to see if all have put their names on their papers before they are collected.

| MANAGEMENT PROBLEM: | *QUIET ACTIVITIES FOR INDEPENDENT WORK* |

MANAGEMENT PROBLEM: *QUIET ACTIVITIES FOR INDEPENDENT WORK*

TEACHER'S CONCERN: What are some quiet activities for children to do while waiting for others to finish work?

WORKABLE OPTIONS:

1. Students draw profiles and cut out pictures to paste on the profile that reflect their feelings/thoughts for that day or that represent their interests (e.g., skiing, hiking, reading, etc.).

2. Provide extra worksheets on areas of learning that have already been covered in class. Children love to do such work alone.

3. Provide books, videos, tape recorders, use of computer software, and puzzle materials for individual activities (interest corners).

4. Create an art box with extra art supplies. Children can create independent projects.

5. Provide projects such as hook rugs, pot holders, and ongoing creative materials.

6. Have a sheet of paper headed "I'm happiest when _____" and other incomplete sentences for students to complete.

7. Provide a worksheet with scrambled sentences and words.

8. Provide material for word searches.

9. Fill a reading bag with fun-to-read material such as classic comic books, greeting cards, and riddles.

10. Provide a class scrapbook for students to review.

11. Encourage the recording of information into daily diaries.

MANAGEMENT PROBLEM: *RIVALRY TOWARD PEERS*

TEACHER'S CONCERN: How can I help students improve in their cooperative behavior with peers?

WORKABLE OPTIONS:

1. Try to identify the factors within the classroom environment that may be contributing to the student's resentment (e.g., no friends, not enough positive attention, ridiculed by peers because of some idiosyncrasy, etc.).

2. Talk to teachers who have taught the student in the past to obtain information about the student's sensitivity while working with his peers.

3. Give the student classroom responsibilities so that he may gain respect from the other students.

4. Encourage the student to talk to his classmates in a cooperative manner.

5. Talk with the student privately to help him see the kinds of problems he is creating with his peers.

6. Provide many occasions for the student to gain positive emotional support from his peers (e.g., group projects).

7. Get the student involved in peer tutoring so that he has firsthand experience with individual differences.

8. Use a peer rating procedure to determine the relative popularity of each student in the class. A sociogram is an excellent procedure.

MANAGEMENT PROBLEM:	*SHORT ATTENTION SPAN*

TEACHER'S CONCERN: How can I manage students who have a very short attention span and find it very difficult to concentrate?

WORKABLE OPTIONS:

1. Check to see if the student has had a good breakfast and a good night's rest (Maslow's basic needs).

2. Use the services of school personnel to see if the student has any physical problems.

3. Make sure the lesson includes visual, auditory, and motor activities. Be sensitive to the student's area of strength within the multiple intelligences (Howard Gardner).

4. Check to see that worksheets are neat, clear, and interesting to the students.

5. Use a cardboard carrel so that the student can better attend to what he is doing and not be distracted.

6. Avoid seating the student next to the window, the fish tank, the class pet, or near the door where hall activity can be observed.

7. Attention span may be increased if a motor activity is included, such as reading a story and then acting out the parts, or making something to illustrate the story (hands-on activity).

8. For the lower grades, have short learning periods alternating with short activities so that the day is fast paced and varied.

MANAGEMENT PROBLEM:	*SILENT CHILD*

TEACHER'S CONCERN: How can I relate to a silent child who does not react positively or negatively to compliments or complaints?

WORKABLE OPTIONS:

1. If you consider the behavior serious, ask the Child Study Team to examine the situation.

2. Even if initially unsuccessful, continue to relate in a positive way to the child. This may eventually lead to a better relationship with the child.

3. Try to discover what interests the child has and then offer an opportunity to do some independent work in this area. Partner this child with another who is more outgoing but sensitive.

4. Request a conference with the child's parent(s) and ask for their opinions or ideas.

5. Use a class sociogram technique to find out who the child would like to be with or considers a friend in the classroom. Seat them near each other. Perhaps a friendship will develop and the other child will be a good model.

6. Utilize the services of a counselor if such services are available in your school.

7. If the child is able and willing, give him a task that would assure success (e.g., ask the child to design and put up the next bulletin board and select other classmates to assist him). This project may open up the lines of communication between you and the student.

MANAGEMENT PROBLEM:	*SITTING IN SEAT*

TEACHER'S CONCERN:

What do I do with a student who is constantly out of his seat, putting his feet in the aisle, and stretching across his chair rather than sitting in it?

WORKABLE OPTIONS:

1. Set clear rules as to what is expected during academic periods.

2. Discuss safety rules and consequences of improper use of one's chair or putting one's feet in the aisle.

3. Place a student who has difficulty sitting still closer to your desk.

4. Whenever possible, reward for correct behavior, even if it is only for a short period of time (e.g., send him on an errand, allow him/her to get a drink of water, etc.).

5. Be sure he has had a physical and has no health problems that make sitting still difficult (or impossible).

6. Try to ignore some behaviors and concentrate on students who are working well. This provides a model for the student who doesn't sit quietly and may encourage correct behavior.

7. Role play a classroom, with you being the student. Show examples of some of the habits the students' exhibit and discuss them. Often very young students are not aware of this behavior and seeing it helps them understand the problem.

8. Provide adequate opportunity for movement around the classroom. Extended sitting in a desk is difficult for anyone, but may be nearly impossible for the very young.

MANAGEMENT	
PROBLEM:	*SOCIAL ADJUSTMENT OF NEW STUDENT*

TEACHER'S
CONCERN: What can I do to help the social adjustment of a new student in my class?

WORKABLE
OPTIONS:

1. Develop a class sociogram. Determine the popular students and select one who will agree to be the class host and show new students around the school.

2. Have the class share their answers to an open statement such as "The proudest time in my life was _____." Be sure the new student shares his answer with the class.

3. After getting to know a little about the new student, have each student write four positive observations about him. Read these aloud and let him keep them as a welcome to the class.

4. Have the students pair up, answer one or two questions given by you, and then switch partners. These questions should probe attitudes, which will allow the students to get to know one another.

5. Make available to the student or his parents the school handbook or catalog that provides the school's rules and regulations, floor plan with location of classes, information about the cafeteria, etc.

6. In the beginning, participate in the students' activities during recess to see that the new student is included.

7. Be friendly and accepting of the new student. If the students have seen your acceptance, it may be easier for them to do the same.

8. Don't pressure the new student to adjust. Let him move at his own pace.

MANAGEMENT PROBLEM:	*STEALING*

TEACHER'S CONCERN: What do I do when things are being taken from other students in the class? I ask the class to find it, and one student always finds what is missing. What do I do with students caught stealing?

WORKABLE OPTIONS:

1. For the student who always finds what is missing, it might be prudent to quietly go to that student's desk after someone has reported something missing, and ask the student for it. Having him "find" it each time is giving him attention and positive feedback for a negative action.

2. Discuss with the class the consequences of stealing in the outside world. A trip to the county jail, courthouse, or police station may be enlightening. A visit from a local policeman who will discuss the topic is also helpful.

3. Instruct the students to keep valuables in a safe place. Discourage bringing valuables to school. Give them the option of giving you valuables (change from lunch money, computer toys, etc.) for safekeeping until the end of the day.

4. Refer to a potentially stolen article as "lost" and ask students to "find" it.

5. Allow for privacy in returning "lost articles" so that you will have an opportunity to talk directly to the student.

6. Contact and inform parents if it is habitual behavior.

7. Explore the child's motive for stealing. Reasons such as poverty, attention, and desire need to be addressed, and alternate means of meeting these needs should be determined.

| MANAGEMENT PROBLEM: | *STEALING SCHOOL PROPERTY* |

MANAGEMENT PROBLEM: *STEALING SCHOOL PROPERTY*

TEACHER'S CONCERN: What kind of measures can I take to discourage students from stealing school property?

WORKABLE OPTIONS:

1. Provide classroom activities that expose students to the underlying principles of the property rights of others (e.g., films, video, computer software, short stories, copyrights. etc. through class discussions, role playing, and research).

2. Try to determine the cause of stealing by privately talking to the student (e.g., uncontrollable urge, a lack of basic necessities, revenge upon others, forgetfulness, lack of a sense of responsibility, etc.).

3. Require that the student return the stolen object or reimburse the owner.

4. When students steal repeatedly, they should be severely reprimanded, the parents should be notified, and recommendations for counseling and review by the Child Study Team should be considered.

5. Students who cannot directly return the item or immediately reimburse the owner should be required to "work off" the amount and/or have the exact sum deducted from their weekly allowances or wages.

6. Emphasize the importance of a sense of trust among peers, the need to respect others, and general discussions on alternative methods of obtaining desired materials.

7. Make the students aware, through discussion or by publishing in the school policy handbook, the consequences of taking school property. Follow up on the consequences consistently.

MANAGEMENT PROBLEM: *STORAGE SPACE FOR MINIMAL COST*

TEACHER'S CONCERN: How can I increase storage space for students and myself?

WORKABLE OPTIONS:

1. Obtain large cardboard boxes from stores. Decorate with attractive coverings. These may be stacked or lined up depending on what is stored inside.

2. Make a class building project. Use cinder blocks and boards to make bookshelves.

3. Purchase inexpensive metal shelving of various heights from hardware stores. Be sure they are firmly placed so that they do not fall over and injure the teacher or children.

4. To store gym clothes and similar items, make duffel bags to be hung in the closet.

5. Enlist the help of the vocational-technical high school. Many times classes are eager to make projects such as shelves, closets, tables, etc.

6. Check your closets for out-of-date materials and tools you no longer use.

7. Catalog and organize all your materials so they are efficiently placed for strategic use.

8. Set an example for the students of an organized, neat classroom and follow this up with monthly "clean-outs" of desks and backpacks.

MANAGEMENT PROBLEM:	*STUDENT ARGUES AND DENIES INVOLVEMENT IN A NEGATIVE ACTION*
TEACHER'S CONCERN:	A student is corrected for doing something wrong and becomes sarcastic. What do I do when he denies the action for which he was clearly responsible?
WORKABLE OPTIONS:	

1. Check to see if the discipline technique being used is too harsh or unfair.

2. Check to see if you are being consistent in your discipline for all students.

3. Do not confront the student in front of the group, which will put him on the defensive.

4. Don't make threats that cannot be carried out, such as "You will never go out to recess again." The student may lose respect for the teacher or not take the discipline seriously.

5. Clarify exactly what disruptive behavior the student has exhibited and what the consequences will be.

6. Be firm in your voice tone, facial expressions, and gestures.

7. Highly praise a student who takes the consequences of disruptive behavior in a mature manner.

8. If a student is having a problem maintaining control, have a time out period for him to settle down before you continue to discuss concerns.

9. Role play arguments and discuss reactions.

10. Control your emotions so that you can rationally respond to the problem at hand.

MANAGEMENT PROBLEM:	*STUDENT CRITICISM*

TEACHER'S CONCERN: What can I do when students constantly criticize each other?

WORKABLE OPTIONS:

1. Have a classroom discussion concerning the students who are constantly criticizing each other. Be honest and show how it negatively affects the classroom atmosphere. Give the students an opportunity to share their feelings and concerns. Then give the students the responsibility of finding or developing solutions to this problem.

2. Through role play, share various techniques for expressing feelings without criticizing the person with whom you are communicating.

3. Many times the students who criticize or tease other students have low self-esteem. Therefore, try to create an atmosphere where everyone feels important, but not more important than anyone else in the class. This could be done by equally sharing the numerous responsibilities that lead to successful learning experiences in the classroom.

4. Try the following activity. Have the students sit in groups of five. Each student tells about himself, and the other students list three positive attributes after listening to him (thoughtful, sincere, artistic, talented, etc.). Each student shares these observations with the student who has just spoken. This demands that students find something positive about each other rather than something sarcastic and negative. It is often helpful to list positive words on the board (suggested by students) to help the students get into the "mood." This is especially effective with teenagers who find it difficult to express positive comments about each other.

MANAGEMENT PROBLEM:	*STUDENT HAS PERSONAL PROBLEM THAT SEEMS TO INTERFERE WITH HIS PROGRESS, BUT HE HAS NOT SHARED THIS INFORMATION WITH THE TEACHER*

TEACHER'S CONCERN:

How can I help this student with his problem if he has not shared the problem with me?

WORKABLE OPTIONS:

1. Seek out the help of the guidance counselor and see if he has some information that can help you.

2. Check with the members of the Child Study Team and see if they can help you understand some of the student's concerns without infringing on the confidentiality to which the student is entitled.

3. Have a conference with the student to see if he can talk about what you feel is interfering with his academic progress.

4. Have a conference with the parents expressing your concern about the student and offering your support and assistance.

5. Encourage discussion of concerns and problems through formal and informal group sessions.

6. Do not pressure the student to reveal personal concerns that he/she does not wish to reveal. Work on building a rapport of trust and confidence with the student. When he is ready, he will share the problem with you.

7. The student may be suffering extreme stress and is reluctant to bring it to the teacher's attention feeling it might show weakness. An effective technique used is to have your students construct a small red flag attached to a suction stick (obtained at any craft store) which can be placed on their desk if they wish to speak to the teacher personally or need help from their peer aide. It actually works by providing an unobtrusive contact signal that assures acknowledgement.

MANAGEMENT PROBLEM:	*STUDENT WHO WORKS ACCURATELY BUT MORE RAPIDLY THAN OTHERS*
TEACHER'S CONCERN:	How do I cope with children who complete all work given to them in a minimal amount of time?

WORKABLE OPTIONS:

1. Evaluate appropriateness of assignments. Determine whether this student needs more challenging work.

2. Use an art box consisting of old art and material scraps. Such items fascinate children and help keep them busy. Make this box accessible to elementary level children upon completion of work.

3. Use learning centers such as "Things I Want to Know." Children supply questions and answers to each other's queries.

4. Establish a game area. Provide crossword puzzles on poster boards, jigsaw puzzles, potholder making, hook rugs, etc. Provide activities that can be left and resumed easily at another time.

5. Provide a personal evaluation sheet. Such a sheet includes individual goals that the teacher would like the child to achieve. The child grades himself after completion of each task. The teacher reviews this sheet at the end of each week and the child is rewarded for progress and independent work.

6. Provide a folder in some area of the room containing extra worksheets from assignments already completed. Let students select ones they like and work independently.

7. Allow these students to work on an independent project that involves the use of the library. When work is completed, students can request a library pass so that they may go to the library and do research on their project.

MANAGEMENT PROBLEM:	*STUDENT WHO WORKS INACCURATELY AND RUSHES THROUGH ASSIGNMENTS*
TEACHER'S CONCERN:	How can I control the tendency to work too quickly, but not accurately?

WORKABLE OPTIONS:

1. Assign small quantities of work. Large amounts tend to make the children rush to accomplish all they are given to do.

2. Establish expected and realistic time limits for activities. This will take the pressure off the child.

3. Do sample lessons with the children to help them learn to pace themselves while working.

4. Use bar graphs to indicate the length of time taken to complete an activity. Emphasize that the one who finishes first is not the winner in this game. It is the one who finishes correctly!

5. Discuss the consequences of working too quickly.

6. Attach an undesirable task to an assignment completed carelessly (e.g., rewriting).

7. Reward work prepared carefully with stickers or seals.

8. Do some work with the class to show the difference between quality and quantity of work. Relate this to shopping in the store (e.g., Would you like to buy five rotten oranges for 10 cents, or one large good one for 10 cents?).

9. Establish reasonable time schedules with the class.

MANAGEMENT PROBLEM:	*STUDENTS RUSHING TO LEAVE ROOM WHEN BELL RINGS*

TEACHER'S CONCERN: What I dislike the most is when students pack up their book bags before class is even over in anticipation of the end-of-period bell. What can I do to stop that?

WORKABLE OPTIONS:

1. Simply make it a class rule that students are not permitted to pack up their book bags until you say it is time to do so. Also explain and discuss your reasoning for this rule.

2. When the students do this consistently, it may mean that they do not value the last five or ten minutes of the class. You may want to evaluate your lesson planning and make the end of your teaching period more meaningful to the students.

3. On some of your tests, allow the students to use their notes. Then the students will be aware of the value of good note taking that represents the entire class period.

4. Inform the students that a part of the grade for the course will reflect how well the classroom time is utilized.

5. It is not unusual for freshmen to be apprehensive about the time allotted in moving from one class to another. Assure these students that you will dismiss them in time to get to their next class. Often these students carry every book they need for the day in their backpack because they are afraid of being late for their next class. It is important that you take this into consideration and assure them that you will not extend the period and make them late for their next class!

6. Practice your timing so that your lesson is not rushed at the end of the period.

MANAGEMENT	
PROBLEM:	*SUBSTITUTE TEACHERS*

**TEACHER'S
CONCERN:** How can I be assured that the substitute reads and follows the plans I have left for him?

**WORKABLE
OPTIONS:**

1. Work out an arrangement with the main office so that the substitute will be given your plans immediately upon entering the building.

2. Include a cover sheet with your lesson plans. On the cover sheet, print: "Please read lesson plans in entirety." Also include an evaluation sheet that permits the substitute to check off the areas covered with spaces for remarks on how well the students performed in each area, as well as a list of certain students who may need extra help and suggestions.

3. Include your schedule and material list.

4. Prior to your absence, arrange with a neighboring teacher, familiar with your schedule, to look in on your class.

5. Appoint student helpers. List their names for the substitute, as well as the duties for which they are responsible (e.g., giving out or collecting papers, being a line leader, etc.).

6. Maintain an organized classroom. Keep all teaching materials accessible to the substitute.

7. Establish a daily routine. Adhere to it. Such familiarity with a schedule will help the children be more comfortable with a substitute who follows the established schedule.

8. Establish a set of behaviors you feel constitutes proper management, and reinforce these expectations with the students. Students will understand that these rules are important in building a productive learning environment.

MANAGEMENT PROBLEM:	*TALKING IN THE CLASSROOM*

TEACHER'S CONCERN:

What do I do with students who continuously talk when they should be listening or working?

WORKABLE OPTIONS:

1. Give a warning or warning signal (e.g., flicking the lights on and off). Then if talking persists, withhold a reward or give a punishment.

2. Occasionally reward or punish the entire class. Peer pressure is a powerful force.

3. Try a strict behavior modification program. (See "A Ticket To Elementary Classroom Management Success," pp. 113-115 in Section II of this booklet.)

4. Discuss the importance of not talking and why talking is not allowed.

5. At the beginning of the school year, establish a time when talking is not allowed.

6. Allow students free time to chat. This may cut down on the talking out of turn.

7. During seatwork time, allow students to communicate through writing notes or whispering. Abuse of this privilege will result in some predetermined consequence.

8. Use proximity to get right in the middle of the classroom, possibly touching a noisy student's shoulder to keep class discussion flowing without bringing peer attention to this student.

9. Confer with parents and help them establish a reward system for good days.

10. Separate talkers so the temptation is reduced.

11. Provide lessons on manners, respect, etc.

MANAGEMENT PROBLEM:	*TANTRUMS*
TEACHER'S CONCERN:	How do I deal with a child who is throwing a tantrum (i.e., pushing his desk or books, screaming, crying, throwing objects, etc.)?

WORKABLE OPTIONS:

1. At the first indication of this radical behavior, go to the child and put your hand on his shoulder to calm him down.

2. If he continues to be out of control, remove him from the classroom for the protection of other children

3. Refer the child to the school disciplinarian or counselor as there may be a Board policy for handling this extreme problem.

4. After the student has left, discuss with the other students proper behavior in the classroom and why it is expected for each student.

5. Students can brainstorm to provide alternative behaviors that are acceptable in dealing with disappointments, anger, frustration, etc.

6. Check into what caused the tantrum and try to structure the environment so that a tantrum is not triggered again. Be tolerant, flexible, understanding, and caring.

7. Attach a consequence. Make sure the frequency (severity) of the offense is in direct proportion to the severity of the consequence. Keep an accurate record of when and why the tantrum happened and other details.

8. Contact the parents. Try to obtain feedback on how they feel about this and their ideas on what causes this behavior. (Medication, sudden flare-ups.)

9. See the PBS Video film *How Difficult Can it Be.*

MANAGEMENT PROBLEM:	*TARDINESS*

TEACHER'S CONCERN: What alternative strategies can I implement when a student's frequent tardiness disrupts the class?

WORKABLE OPTIONS:

1. Talk to the student privately to see if there is a valid reason for his tardiness.

2. Explain to students what measures will be taken if repeated violations occur.

3. Praise the students for their promptness (e.g., "It's nice to see that everyone arrived to class before the bell!").

4. Reward students for their promptness by allowing them to participate in a special weekly activity (e.g., listening to tapes, playing games, etc.).

5. Use group contingencies when several or more students are arriving late for class (e.g., "If all students enter the room before the bell rings, then the class will be able to watch a video during quiet time").

6. Take from a student's free time the amount of time that he is late for class (e.g., five minutes late means that the student stays five minutes extra).

7. Students who are excessively late (more than ten or fifteen minutes) and/or continually late for no apparent reason should be required to double the time that they must make up for their lateness.

8. Contact parents about the student's tardiness.

9. Inform the principal or school counselor about students who are chronically late for a follow-up.

| MANAGEMENT PROBLEM: | *TEACHER STRESS* |

MANAGEMENT PROBLEM: *TEACHER STRESS*

TEACHER'S CONCERN: How can I deal with the stress that I encounter as a classroom teacher?

WORKABLE OPTIONS:

1. Stress is not a problem, but rather a symptom. Focus on what is causing the stress. It may be classroom management, administrative pressure, lack of community support, home responsibilities, or lack of sleep, but the important decision is to take action. The appropriate action for each specific situation can be found in other sections of this publication.

2. If the stress is extreme, seek professional assistance.

3. It is possible that you have "maxed out" in your teaching skills and need a change. Investigate other professional areas in and out of education. Such a change can bring back the enthusiasm you once felt as a classroom teacher.

4. When experiencing a stressful situation, write down in a log the situation and how you are dealing with it. After a period of time, evaluate the log and see if a pattern develops. This information will assist you in making appropriate changes in your teaching.

5. When experiencing anxiety, share your feelings with the people with whom you are dealing. This may lower your level of stress after an incident.

6. Make a concerted effort to separate your stress-producing problems and handle them one at a time. Once you have coped with one situation, that success often alleviates other situations that have led to a stressful reaction.

7. Evaluate your reactions and be sure you are not overreacting to the responsibilities placed upon you. You cannot solve everyone's problems!

MANAGEMENT	
PROBLEM:	*TELEVISION AND THE INTERNET*

TEACHER'S
CONCERN: It seems to me that the students watch too much television and spend too much time "surfing the Net." Is there anything I can do about this?

WORKABLE
OPTIONS:

1. Have a meeting with the parents to ask for their opinions and suggestions for solving this problem.

2. Although it is a value judgment, assist the students in selecting some of the shows they watch on TV and the amount of time they spend "surfing the Net." This may improve the quality of the programs they watch and a more thoughtful selection of Internet materials.

3. Discuss with the students other types of activities they could experience and enjoy.

4. Ask the students to record the number of hours they watch television or spend their computer each week. Also have them list what else they do during that week. Have cooperative learning groups develop an evaluative scale to measure the quality use of their time.

5. Introduce the students to other community activities and services available to them. Bring in speakers to present these options.

6. Have books available in the classroom that represent areas of the students' interest. Have weekly book reviews where students discuss the concepts of stories they have read. Initiate a paperback book exchange.

7. Have students choose a program and write an evaluative review using a general questionnaire. "What have you learned? How was the quality of acting? Was it realistic and believable? Did it discuss a positive or negative aspect of life?"

MANAGEMENT PROBLEM:	*TRUANCY*

TEACHER'S CONCERN:

How can I improve my students' attitudes toward school when the reasons for their poor attendance are boredom, non-caring attitude, and peer pressure?

WORKABLE OPTIONS:

1. Plan class trips through the community and/or to public buildings, parks, and historical sites to make school as interesting as possible for the students.

2. Try to motivate the student to get involved in constructive athletics or club activities where others depend upon his being present.

3. Make adjustments in the student's program whenever possible (e.g., late arrival, early dismissal, half day schedule, etc.) and if requested by the Child Study Team or counselor. Be flexible. Let the student know how pleased you are to have him/her in your class. Be sincere!

4. Begin a reward system to reinforce when the student comes to school (e.g., "Each day you are in school, you will receive a credit toward a special weekly activity of your own choosing.").

5. Provide individual counseling for the student to discover why he avoids school.

6. Send a registered letter to the parents noting weekly school absences (after you have tried to contact them by telephone and if it is school policy). Note the legal consequences of truancy.

7. Contact the school attendance officer for a home visit if the problem becomes severe.

8. Give a monthly report to the administration and/or supervisors about students who have an excessive number of absences (e.g., 10 or more days absent in a given time period).

SECTION II

A TEACHER-TESTED ELEMENTARY CLASSROOM MANAGEMENT SYSTEM

A TICKET TO ELEMENTARY CLASSROOM MANAGEMENT SUCCESS

A. INTRODUCTION

This is a recipe for positive reinforcement based on a ticket system that rewards acceptable behavior and penalizes unacceptable behavior. This allows the students to clearly identify right from wrong and provides them the opportunity to correct a wrongdoing and change unacceptable behavior into acceptable behavior.

B. OBJECTIVES

With the implementation of this program the students will be able to:

* Identify and respond to basic classroom rules
* Establish parameters clarifying these rules to help prevent them from stepping "over the line" and getting penalized for breaking rules they did not know
* Demonstrate an awareness of self-worth, self-respect, and self-discipline
* Demonstrate an understanding of the outcome of both positive and negative behavior
* Demonstrate sensitivity and awareness of the need to respect others

C. BASIC COMPONENTS

To implement this program, it is necessary to understand the basic components that allow the teacher to demonstrate clearly to the students whether or not they have successfully fulfilled the behavioral requirements so important to building a productive learning environment. The procedure is as follows:

On the first day of school (or whenever introducing the system), post on the blackboard or on a bulletin board the following clarifying information:

> **Green ticket**—Positive behavior
> **Gold ticket**—Value of 10 green tickets
> **Silver ticket**—Issued for earning 10 gold tickets

Upon receipt of the **silver** ticket, the student is recognized as Student of the Month in the classroom.

Other tickets in the system are:

> **Red ticket**—Unacceptable behavior
> **Black ticket**—Issued after 5 red tickets

The **black** ticket leads to detention.

In addition to the ticket system, supportive rewards for the students are provided as follows:

1. A Reward Box with things in it that the student may reach in and "grab" after receipt of a **gold** ticket.
2. An **ice cream** ticket when the **silver** ticket is achieved (often cost is provided by PTA).
3. A mystery gift when a second **silver** ticket is received (donated by local merchants).
4. A chance surprise when withdrawing color tickets from ticket box.

D. PROCESS

All behavior is judged on concrete and tangible activities of the students. This includes class conduct and homework. The student's effort is the primary indicator of his/her success or failure to receive tickets. There is no misunderstanding regarding right and wrong for this is clearly defined throughout the day in all activities.

When the teacher calls the roll at the beginning of each day, the student rates his conduct of the previous day. When a student's name is called, he replies "yes" if his conduct was acceptable and "no" if his conduct was unacceptable.

The same procedure applies to homework, with the students responding "complete" or "incomplete."

On the front of each student's desk is a plastic holder into which the earned tickets are placed each day. These tickets are displayed for everyone to see.

If a student answers "yes" and "complete" all week, he has received a green ticket for each day. On Friday his name goes up on the Honors Bulletin Board.

The student achieving a "yes" and "complete" for an entire month receives a certificate signed and issued by the principal.

E. MATERIALS

Tickets are 2"×2" squares cut from the appropriate color construction paper and kept in a shoe box marked with the respective colors (green, gold, red, or black). As each student earns a ticket, as an added incentive, he picks from the appropriate box without looking. If the student picks a green ticket with a smiling face stamped on it, the student is then eligible to pick a "grabber" with different fun things in them, such as permission to be first in line, skip an assignment, etc.

If the class receives a compliment from anyone other than the classroom teacher (specials, principal, visitor) they get two green tickets. They also can lose a green ticket if they do something unacceptable, but they may earn it back by improved behavior. Anyone getting a red ticket can work it off by doing what he did wrong correctly, such as not calling out in class or annoying another student.

Certificates awarded can be easily designed with any print computer software.

F. SUMMARY BY CREATOR OF SYSTEM

"I have used this system for over 13 years and it works better every year. Once it gets started it is so motivating that within weeks, red tickets are no longer needed. Everyone's day is usually pleasant and happy, and the students become very aware and sensitive to the needs of others."

A Way of Life
Know how to have respect for myself and others…
Involve myself as an active and good citizen…
Never lie or hurt others…
Do to others what you want them to do to you…

Discipline is a mode of learning that demonstrates positive and moral behavior. Discipline reflects the three basic concepts:

1. Love your students.
2. Trust your students.
3. Be gentle but firm in your classroom management.

"It takes love, consistency and record keeping everyday, but the rewards for the teacher and students are so fulfilling it is worth the extra effort."

> —*Ann Weinbrenner, classroom teacher, Long Beach Island Consolidated School District*

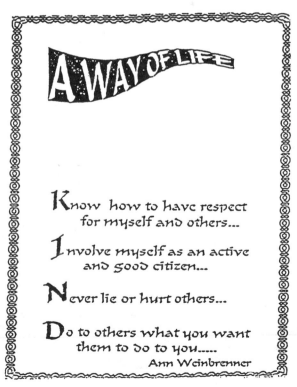

SECTION III

ADDITIONAL SPECIFIC MANAGEMENT SUGGESTIONS PROVIDED BY MIDDLE AND SECONDARY SCHOOL TEACHERS

**MANAGEMENT
PROBLEM:** *ACTING OUT*

**TEACHER'S
CONCERN:** What do I do with students who are constantly interrupting the class by acting out?

**WORKABLE
OPTIONS:**

1. Be sure to check to see if the work is too difficult for them. If this is the case, assign them a student peer who could be of help or plan to work with them privately during a period of the day when you provide student assistance.

2. Check to see if their behavior is based on a desire for more attention from you or recognition from their classmates. If these are the reasons, make a point of calling on these students to do things around the classroom that keep them busy and makes them feel useful.

3. *Never ever* respond to students' acting out in front of the entire class. Move around as you teach and make a point of spending time beside the student's desk who is acting out, touching his shoulder or in some way acknowledging that you are aware that what he is doing is inappropriate. By making an issue of his actions you are validating them and responding to his desire to "be cool in front of his peers."

4. Review the "*Motivational Theory*" presented in this booklet for additional suggestions to respond to this behavior (pp. 129–142).

MANAGEMENT PROBLEM:	*GOSSIPING*

TEACHER'S CONCERN:	How do I deal with the gossiping that goes on in class?

WORKABLE OPTIONS:

1. When gossip is observed, privately discuss with the two or more offending students what they are doing and how harmful and hurtful this can be. Encourage them to decide on and implement alternative actions that would mend the harm they have done and be more sensitive about being critical of others.

2. Have a general brief lesson regarding what is gossip and what is truth. Have students follow up this discussion by developing personal rules regarding the appropriate way to interact with their peers, their neighbors, and adults. In English subject classes this would be a meaningful lesson dealing with communication skills. The essays could be bound and placed in the library acknowledging the class that wrote it. Suggest to the librarian about having a section exclusively for student-made books. A great idea!

3. Provide a role-playing experience as a special activity in the classroom using "gossiping" as the theme. Students enjoy the opportunity to present their ideas. It will also act as an icebreaker for less-verbal students or those new to the school.

4. Set a good example and do not gossip about other teachers or parents. It is never appropriate, even in the teachers' room! Teachers at all levels of education must represent the best in personal qualities. It is vital that what is heard or discussed with your colleagues be kept within the professional community and hopefully not discussed at all if it is hearsay or hurtful to anyone.

MANAGEMENT PROBLEM:	*LACK OF MOTIVATION*

TEACHER'S CONCERN: How do I encourage unmotivated students to participate more willingly and more enthusiastically in class activities?

WORKABLE OPTIONS:

1. Assign weekly jobs to give these students an active role in the management of the classroom. This serves two purposes: it requires student attendance throughout the week to fulfill the responsibility and helps the student become personally involved in the classroom work. Some secondary teachers will argue that this is a task for elementary students, but secondary students also enjoy being teacher assistant in fulfilling chores such as taking attendance, collecting papers, distributing materials, and acting as a peer assistant. This also saves a lot of time from the teacher's day that could be used more productively.

2. Be sure you have planned your lesson well so that less time is wasted on explaining the work to be done, providing the materials needed to complete the work, and clearly designating within the lesson how the student can get help with material not understood (e.g., peer partners, location of resource material).

3. Have available extra pencils, pens, papers, staplers, etc. on a work table so students can take and use what they need and do not interrupt the lesson.

4. Acknowledge a student working appropriately so others can see what appropriate behavior is!

5. A ninth-grade teacher suggested having some sort of sustenance for the students especially in the last afternoon classes. She provides a bowl of popcorn and water bottles on a table in the rear of the room. She explains that she has observed students are often tired or hungry and this affects their attention span and their ability to concentrate, which can be misinterpreted as lack of motivation.

MANAGEMENT PROBLEM:	*NOISY WORK AND BEHAVIOR HABITS*

TEACHER'S CONCERN:	How should I handle students who have noisy work habits and are generally noisy when moving to classes during school?

WORKABLE OPTIONS:

1. Point out the fact that other classroom doors are open and lessons are going on.

2. Explain how important it is for the students to focus on the lesson, stay on task, and continue doing their best.

3. Discuss with the class the appropriate behavior in the hallway when changing classes.

4. During homeroom, provide a map of the school so that students will be aware of the most direct way to get to their next class. Discuss this so that plans for moving up and down the appropriate stairways can be arranged.

5. During group activity or individual work experiences in the classroom, emphasize the proper means of communication among students (soft voices and limited movement around the room so other students are not disturbed).

6. Designate various areas in the classroom for active verbal activity separated with barriers to avoid disturbing the individual students working quietly on their own assignments.

7. Designate the signal to be used when students need help during a quiet work period, such as a raised hand or a flag on the desk (see *Motivational Theory*, pp. 129–142).

8. Praise the student working appropriately without disturbing others.

MANAGEMENT PROBLEM:	*PLAGIARISM*

TEACHER'S CONCERN: With information so easily accessible on the Internet, how do I discourage and prevent plagiarism by my students?

WORKABLE OPTIONS:

1. The importance of honesty in presenting materials is a vital area to be discussed and understood by students. It is possible to check on the Internet to see if some material has been plagiarized, but it is more important to make clear to your students that any borrowed material (e.g., from an article, book, public presentation, the news, etc.) should include the source. Plagiarism of anything can result in drastic consequences throughout a student's life (e.g., reports, résumés, etc.).

2. In a mock discussion, acknowledge as your own an idea submitted by a student. Identify the student and ask how he felt when his idea was "stolen." This can lead to an interesting discussion.

3. Explain copyright laws or have students research the laws that clearly define plagiarism as illegal.

4. When assigning research papers, review the rules of footnotes and the procedures to be followed in providing accurate bibliographies.

5. Help students develop their personal résumés. Demonstrate the importance of accurate information. Provide examples of persons in high places that have lost positions because of inaccuracies on their résumés.

6. Have students develop a brief essay on the phrase "Honesty is the best policy" and share their comments with the class.

MANAGEMENT	
PROBLEM:	*REBELLION*

TEACHER'S
CONCERN: In several of my classes, I have small groups of students who seem to go out of their way to be and look different. I realize that this is a stage they are going through, but with all the aggression, police in the hallways, and especially the Columbine incident, I wonder when I need to step in to express my displeasure or even alert administration to my concerns?

WORKABLE
OPTIONS:

1. No one can deny that today's school climate presents new and possibly dangerous concerns. Your question is a serious one. As a classroom teacher you have the right to expect acceptable behavior in your classroom, as well as in the school in general. *It is extremely important* that you do not judge the student solely by his appearance and assume that if he wears an earring in his nose, on his tongue, or some other place on his body, *he is a rebellious student.* The "packaging" does not always indicate the quality of the "gift." If the student is attentive, does his work as assigned, participates in class, and in general is considered cooperative and involved in the job of learning, his adornments should not be misleading.

2. In contrast, if the student is sullen in his behavior, reluctant to participate in class activities, isolates himself from anyone other than his tight group of friends, and is quick to anger, it is important that he and his friends be referred to the school counselor or psychologist for group counseling. There is need, in this day of unreasonable aggression in our schools, to be alert to any possible conflicts that could cause harm to the perpetrator and those around him. Parents should be involved. Refer to the *Motivational Theory* provided in Section IV (pp. 129–142) for specific management ideas.

MANAGEMENT PROBLEM:	*SNICKERING*

TEACHER'S CONCERN: There often seems to be a group of two or three students whispering and snickering off in the corner of the room; this really annoys me and causes a serious distraction to the other students, especially during quiet work time. Any suggestions?

WORKABLE OPTIONS:

1. There are several suggestions to respond to this behavior. For immediate action, move toward the students involved and continue your lesson as you stand there.

2. For follow-up, ask these students to see you immediately after class; if it is a work period, have them come to a quiet place in the room and talk to them about their behavior.

3. For upper grade students, it is very effective to ignore this behavior and spend some time at the beginning of the next lesson discussing appropriate classroom behavior. Make sure you provide regular eye contact with the offending students and on occasion, if appropriate, call upon these students for responses and suggestions.

SECTION IV

A TEACHER-TESTED MIDDLE- AND SECONDARY-CLASSROOM MANAGEMENT SYSTEM

THE MOTIVATIONAL THEORY

A. INTRODUCTION

A management system for the middle and secondary level is quite different from programs developed for the elementary school. The significant difference is that in upper grade instructional programs the classroom teacher has more than 125 students on a daily basis; the elementary teacher meets with the same 15 to 25 students daily. This section suggests techniques that the teacher can use to manage the classroom so he can spend more time teaching rather than disciplining the few students that cause disruptions.

Additionally, in most cases upper level grades do have access to full time counseling services, school disciplinarians, and other specialists. Upper-grade level teachers should be aware of and make use of the services available to them within the school and community.

This section introduces the *Motivational Theory of Classroom Management* developed by the author in response to discipline concerns identified by classroom teachers within Middle and Secondary School programs.

This theory is based upon three basic components:
1. Identifying the behavior that motivates negative actions
2. Developing alternatives to this behavior that will provide the student with positive feedback
3. Reinforcing positive behavior to replace the negative behavior by helping the student change his response to the same stimuli

This theory implies that after recognizing the negative behavior, the teacher will be able to direct student actions toward using this same energy for positive actions. The process is successful when the student feels both academic and social success. It is important to realize that social success more than likely leads to academic success, and vice-versa. *The student who perceives himself as unsuccessful or inferior in either area will probably demonstrate his need for attention or validation as a person in a negative manner or through non-participation in general school activities.* The student may decide that the solution may be to be "good at being bad" to get this attention and even the admiration of his peers as his only source of positive reinforcement. The key to the success of this program is the teacher's ability to direct the student's negative actions toward positive behavior, in the process making the student feel good about himself.

B. OBJECTIVES

By using the suggestions provided in this management program, the student will:

- Have a clearer picture of the acceptable behavior within a middle- and/or secondary-school setting.

- Be involved in an active reward system that will provide the student with incentives to become a more responsible person.
- Be clearly aware of the acceptable rules and regulations within his school
- Have the opportunity to practice appropriate personal management skills that will enhance his ability to become a socially acceptable person in school as well as in his everyday life experiences.

C. BASIC COMPONENTS

This theory is built on the concept that each person is responsible for his own actions and that negative behavior is a learned process that needs to be replaced by positive action. (See works by Howard Gardner, Glasser's *Reality Therapy*, Cantor's *Assertive Discipline Theory* , and other behavioral theorists' works.)

In order to determine what changes need to be made, the teacher has to be aware of specific symptoms that can most likely lead to discipline problems. By keeping accurate notes reflecting the student's behavior and, most importantly, what preceded this behavior, the teacher identifies the "symptoms" that seem to stimulate the problem. The problem can be avoided by reacting to these symptoms appropriately to avert the negative behavior in search of the recognition that usually follows. These symptoms are presented to the reader with descriptors dealing with the reward process that is the heart of the *Motivational Theory.*

Behaviors identified most frequently by secondary school teachers that seem to lead to discipline problems, and the procedures used to respond to them using the *Motivational Theory Concept* include:

1. Lack of concentration or daydreaming
2. Evidence of sleep deprivation or hunger
3. Possible hearing or sight problems
4. Difficulty with grade level of work
5. Peer pressure
6. Absenteeism
7. Cliques or small non-school related groups
8. Fear of school relationships
9. Bullying
10. Physical maturation

Proper responses to these concerns or other symptoms of frustration with learning may lessen or alleviate classroom disruptions to achieve successful participation in classroom activities. The teacher who is sensitive to these and other learning problems will have greater success in meeting the needs of his students. Following are specific logical suggestions, in addition to those found in the first and third sections of this booklet, provided by classroom teachers recognizing these concerns.

Problem: *Lack of Concentration/Daydreaming*

Response:

- Do not place the student next to a window where outside activity would be distracting.

- Avoid placing the student near class displays or distractions (such as an active noisy fish tank in a science class or near an open door that leads to the corridor). It is a fact that some individuals have difficulty ignoring extraneous sounds or movement more than others.

- Partner this student with an organized and structured student who will serve as a model and a source of direction and information.

- Present material and assignments in a clear, concise manner in both written and oral form so that the student can process it correctly. Recognize that there are visual and/or oral learners, and that both should be addressed to provide a fair presentation of materials and assignments.

- Teach from a movable position: walk around the classroom and make a special effort to stand near the student who seems to be daydreaming or who exhibits a lack of concentration.

Problem: *Sleep Deprivation and Hunger*

Response:

- Send the student to the nurse to rest or have a snack if possible.

- Meet with the student privately to determine why he comes to school so tired or hungry. There may be a serious problem at home; or perhaps he is staying up too late watching TV in his room, using his computer, or not taking the time to eat breakfast. If it is the latter, determine whether this is a home management problem, lack of financial resources, or just poor planning on the part of the student.

- Give him a day to "clean up his act" and then clearly determine what alternatives are available to the teacher—such as contacting his parents; alerting the school counselor; or, if it is solely a homework completion problem, the possibility of after-school detention with the teacher to complete his work.

Problem: *Hearing, sight, or Other Physical Difficulty*

Response:

It is amazing how often an intelligent student can learn to cope with sight problems or hearing loss without being detected by parents, teachers, or even doctors. It is extremely important that a student not responding to class stimuli be given a thorough physical examination to check hearing, eyesight, etc. to determine whether he is able to do the fast-paced work demanded in middle and high school, which cannot be as personalized as in the elementary school setting. Students have been misplaced in special classes when the problem was not intelligence level but simply that the student could not see the blackboard clearly or hear the teacher's directions while participating in class.

- A complete medical exam may result in the recommendation that the student be placed closer to the front of the classroom, placed away from light glare, provided glasses, etc., to facilitate a learning climate more conducive to his special learning needs.
- The school nurse should assist the teacher in providing the most appropriate changes in teacher-student interaction to enhance the student's learning environment.

Problem: *Difficulty With Grade Level of Work*

Response:

It is essential that the student be placed in a grade level that provides him with an opportunity to learn. This can be achieved only if it is recognized that he possesses the necessary foundation skills to move on to the new material. At the beginning of each semester, all students should be given a teacher made test that clearly examines whether or not the student is able to meet the challenges of the new class work. This is especially important in today's mobile society where it is not uncommon for a student to move from one community to another where the curriculum is quite different.

- Provide peer tutoring for the student who is not prepared for the level of learning that will be presented in your class. It not only helps the student, but also provides an opportunity for the tutor to review his understanding of the material.
- Consider the possibility of change in class placement by consulting the person in the school who is responsible for this decision
- Schedule a weekly tutor time that is open for students to attend by choice or if the teacher feels they need extra help.

Problem: *Peer Pressure*

Response:

- Partner the student you are concerned about with a student who will be a good model and is recognized in your classroom as a positive person. Pair students who would enjoy each other's company as determined by a class sociogram. (See Educational Psychology sources for details.)
- Provide input in your class that emphasizes the value of self worth as you recognize as many students as possible that do well in class. Find something good to say about each student, no matter how small the deed, so that all the students in the classroom feel the joy of success and learning. Peer acceptance is a vital component during the teenage years.

Problem: *Skipping School Without Parental Consent*

Response:

- A student cannot learn if he is not present in the classroom. It is important that you make your classroom inviting and interesting because you are well prepared and can move swiftly and energetically through a lesson. You are the model. If you show your love for the subject you are teaching, the students will follow your lead. Enthusiasm is contagious. (See additional suggestions presented in this booklet dealing with student responsibility and homework.)

- Be reasonable about homework assignments. Often the reason for not attending is fear of failure and inability to do homework. Investigate why a chronic offender is lax with homework assignments.

- Don't jump to the conclusion that the student doesn't care. Home responsibilities may deter his completion of homework or even attendance at school. Perhaps he has no parental supervision. Perhaps he doesn't understand the work. Homework assignments should be designed for the student and should include work he understands so that it acts as a review and practice. Not all parents are willing to assist the student with homework, nor do all parents understand the work the student in learning. Too much homework is a negative situation. It results in students not having any time for personal needs, friendships, etc.

- Many high school students work after school. This has to be considered when determining the reason why a student does not attend school.

- Share your concerns with the school guidance counselor and the school social worker.

- If the school's truant officer is involved because of extensive absences, be advised of the results of his contact with the home and the parents. The teacher's involvement is evidence of caring, which can make a difference in both parent and student attitude.

Problem: *Cliques Within the School or Other Non-School Related Groups*

Response:

- It is not unusual for students with similar interests to become a tight friendship group with no troubling agenda. But there have been situations in our schools today in which groups have developed because of negative reasons. Teachers and parents need to be aware of signs that all is not well in the actions of these groups, such as:

  Change in dress

  Gradual evidence of lower classroom achievement

  Distancing from other students not a part of the group (This is not to say that this is the only reason for such changes, but it demands prompt attention.)

- Teachers need to ask themselves if they are truly aware of their students' problems as well as the rationale behind changes in their behavior.

133

- Can the school counselor help? Should the parents be involved? What does the school administrator need to know? Have other teachers recognized this behavior among the students in classes that belong to this clique? Perhaps a scheduled meeting with all working with the students to discuss their concerns and review their options would help defuse the misunderstandings or the anger that has developed through their relationship to one another.

- If the school district has a Child Study Team (see descriptor in Introduction), should they be involved?

- Would bringing the identified students together with the faculty and parents be effective?

- Discovering the leader is an absolute must. The student who seems to have the strongest involvement in this aggressive group should be identified and involved with the appropriate staff members to explore the situation.

- This is a relatively new concern that haunts our school corridors. It is vital that those in the position to make a difference do so before tragedy befalls the school population.

Problem: *Fear and Anger*

Today's school community has little resemblance to the schools of yesteryear Technology through the use of computers, the graphic presentations on television, the horrific terrorist attacks and threats around the world, as well as the uncertain economy demanding changes in family priorities, have caused upheavals in the stability of the family structure as well and the interactions within the community as a whole. These events have caused extreme reactions among the older students.

These reactions have been identified as fear and/or anger. Students who are not involved in aggressive groups are fearful of their safety. In some cases, parents have chosen to home school their children so that they will not be exposed to the aggressiveness of other students. In other cases, parents have taken the same path of home schooling to instruct their children in physical defense, animosity toward the laws of our country, and rebellion toward the activities of their peers. The consequences of these decisions are yet to be measured.

Response:

- Awareness is the key factor in creating classroom and social environments that deter particular groups of students from trying to or actually taking control of school management and behavior.

- There should be clearly-defined consequences for inappropriate behavior. Before determining the consequences, students must be able to recognize what is considered negative behavior. Do not assume that they already know! Any student whose behavior infringes upon the rights and freedom of his peers and/or his teachers is considered at fault. The students that do perform well in their relationships need to feel safe from harm—psychological, physical, or emotional—when they are in their classrooms and in school.

- This can be achieved by setting up a system that is followed by all teachers in the school with the same degree of severity and consistency. Cantor's *Assertive Discipline Theory* provides excellent guidelines for implementing a program fulfilling this need. The students need to understand through words and actions that their school is a learning institution. While students are in school and their classrooms they must follow the rules that demonstrate their positive and acceptable interaction with one another. Aside from the usual sporadic disturbances in the classroom that can be easily managed by the attentive teacher, the subtle interactions that threaten the safety of classmates should be addressed and should not be tolerated. The confident and *strong teacher* who exhibits leadership in the classroom makes his position clear to all the students, and in doing so, creates a safe classroom within a productive learning environment.

- *The strong teacher* is identified by his ability to make decisions and follow through with them, even if they are unpopular among some of the students. *A strong teacher* is one who feels comfortable with confrontations and accepts his role as a mature adult who displays confidence in his actions.

- *A strong teacher* is one who loves his students and attempts to see their point of view without giving in to what he feels is wrong just to be accepted by the students. *A strong teacher* is one who is able to admit his mistakes and listen to the suggestions of his students in a calm and non-judgmental way. *A strong teacher* is one who comes to school each day well-prepared to teach, holds no grudges from the day before, and is prepared to start each day with energy, confidence, and enthusiasm; and sets clear, firm, and realistic objectives designed to meet the needs of all his students.

Problem: *Bullying*

Response:

- It has often been recognized that the student who bullies another does so because of a poor self-image. Through bullying, he tries to demonstrate his power, which he believes will make him feel better about himself and gain the respect and admiration of his peers.

- Bullying is a type of rudeness. It is a habit some students develop to acquire recognition and also to avoid responsibility. It is important to understand the reason for the rudeness, and the classroom teacher is in a good position to do so. Teachers do not often respond to rudeness because they feel it gives it credibility. Actually the opposite is usually true. Not only does the rude student need a response that identifies his rudeness, but his peers in the classroom also need to know that his behavior is inappropriate and will not be tolerated.

- Anytime a teacher has an opportunity to confront rudeness, he also has an opportunity to change a person's behavior. Not confronting the student can be considered a sign of approval or weakness, and may even be interpreted as validating the behavior.

- It is not unusual for the bullying student to come from a home or neighborhood where this behavior is the accepted and respected mode of action among peers. The social behavior is limited to where the person stands in the pecking order among his peers or in his "gang" (see discussion on cliques). This is their sole accepted means of communication. Unfortunately, too many students have not experienced the use of proper manners in speech and action at home. The teacher acts as a model by providing proper responses to actions to deter a student from asserting himself by bullying. The common use of "thank you," "please," "I beg your pardon," etc. may at first be observed as uncomfortable or a display of weakness. Its casual use by the classroom teacher gives it credibility.

- In addition, recognizing a kind act performed by a student (picking up a dropped pencil, stepping aside so someone may pass, waiting one's turn rather than interrupting) can change not only the student's behavior and attitude, but the classroom climate in general. It is important to realize that upon leaving high school, lack of proper and polite interaction can negatively affect the future of the student in regard to his employment, success in college, business training, and relationships with others. The student who can replace a bullying demeanor with one that is thoughtful and mannerly will have more chances of gaining acceptance, and respect in whatever place in society he wishes to pursue. A mannerly student should be acknowledged for his behavior—such as "You are quite welcome, Bill"—which makes a student feel that he is of value! All of these suggestions seem so logical, but this is unfortunately an area of education that is neglected more than we would like to admit!

Problem: *Physical Maturation Issues*

Response:

- Throughout middle and high school, students experience uneven physical growth and development over which they have no control. Heredity certainly plays an important role in determining physical structure. The smallest student in class (especially if it is a boy) is often the brunt of hurtful humor and sarcasm by his peers. At the other end of the spectrum is the student whose physical development is "advanced" for his age with body changes not shared by his peers.

- The school nurse or physical education teacher should take some time to discuss these concerns and emphasize that they are normal growth and development issues all students will experience during their teenage years. This should be presented as a positive change; encourage students to accept these changes as an exciting anticipation of new frontiers to be explored and enjoyed.

- It is important to alert students to the fact that physical maturation signals responsibility toward mental maturation; that is, understanding and acting in an acceptable manner as an adult. It is a preview of the future and teaches students how to be acceptable members of the world community. *Adolescence can be a time of discovery and a positive introduction to adulthood. It should not be presented as a time of rebellion and confusion.*

D. PROCESSES AND MATERIALS

Other than these general concerns, a lot more goes on in the classroom that needs the teacher's sensitivity and attention. Thus, we introduce the *Motivational Theory Processes and Materials,* which is based on the concept that motivating students to learn can bring a positive attitude to the classroom. This can be achieved by developing a *reward system* that recognizes progress and achievement and develops a love of learning. The *Motivational Theory* is instrumental in classroom management because it is built upon the concept that using small steps to help students enjoy the experience of success can lead to greater understanding of the importance of positive action. Techniques for achieving positive behavior through a *reward system* are described as follows and have been effectively used by classroom teachers to acknowledge student progress in all grade levels in response to both social and academic behavioral situations.

REWARDS:

Homework
A student with four consecutive days of homework submission receives a free homework pass he can use any day he wishes. As homework is designed for review and practice of material already learned, missing one assignment would not be detrimental to the student's progress. This is an excellent motivational tool because often even the best student finds he does not have time to give full attention to his homework because of demands placed upon him for family or school activities (teams, clubs, etc.). The conscientious student will often stay up late to complete the homework assignment and is then exhausted the next day. The relief of an excused homework assignment is a very positive and sensitive approach used by the classroom teacher.

Grab bag
At the end of the week, students who have not been absent for the week and have contributed to class discussion can select something from the "grab bag," which contains school supplies such as pencils, papers, pens, etc, as well as other gimmicks that students of this age would like to have. Local Dollar Stores are often willing to donate such objects. Some secondary teachers expressed skepticism about this approach but were pleased to see it how positive the students acted when given this choice.

Honor passes
Honor passes can be awarded to students at the discretion of the teacher for behavior, work well done, promptness, or whatever the teacher feels is worthy of special recognition. Accumulated honor passes can be used for various occasions. For example, ten honor passes accumulated as the result of special work can be used by the student to attend a monthly breakfast at a local restaurant on Saturday or an arranged breakfast held in the school sponsored by the PTA or PTO.

Surprisingly, upper class students do opt for this opportunity. It is a great time for the teacher and/or the principal to relax and talk with the students about their future plans, suggestions, etc. outside of the usual classroom environment. It provides the students with a more human view of the person who makes decisions that affect their everyday experiences.

Free Hall Passes
A student who has shown responsibility for his actions can be given a hall pass for one week that allows him the right to leave the room for the bathroom or for other acceptable reasons without asking permission.

Classroom Honor Board
Students achieving a high standard on any work in the class (homework, test, lesson, term papers, etc.) will have their name and work placed on the Honor Board for all to see. An even better idea is to have the Honor Board on the hall bulletin board outside the classroom and changing it weekly so that eventually *all* students see some of their work on display! Students can be assigned to this task. Secondary teachers, especially those who do not have their own room, are notorious for putting up pictures or rules for their classrooms and leaving them up for the entire school year with the excuse that secondary students are not interested in such displays. Not true! Teachers who share a room can share display areas or rotate use of the hall bulletin boards. How much more interesting it would be for their students to see their work on display and to know that even though the teacher has many students, he cares about each of them personally and recognizes their efforts to do well in school! Reluctantly, middle school teachers have used this method and found it not only interesting to students, but also admired by visitors to the school. Principals and Superintendents also found time to acknowledge the fine work the teachers were doing. There is no doubt that this would have an impact on the passing of school budgets when those visiting the school and those on the board feel personally involved with the work of the students. It developed into a win-win situation and now is a common sight in the hallways of these schools.

Students of the Week Award
The student of the week's photo (use a digital camera) recognizes his special achievements—a perfect test paper, an outstanding report submitted, neat and correct homework, appropriate behavior in the classroom, demonstration of good teamwork, etc. These photos should be mounted along the corridor or around the classroom and remain in place for the year. It should be set up so that *every* student will eventually find himself *student of the week* sometime during the year (40 weeks of school with 3 to 4 students getting the award each week would total 120-140 student so that everyone should be recognized.) At the end of the school year, students are given their photo with the comment of their special achievement that merited the award attached to take home.

"See Me" Slip
If a student needs special attention, he should receive a "See Me" slip with the time and date of this appointment. The appointment can be arranged for when the classroom teacher has set aside an hour or more a week to meet with students when many of them have study hall or other free time. If this is not possible for some

students, the teacher can have the student list times when he is free and try to group students together to accommodate this. This time should be used to acknowledge improvement in work, an especially outstanding paper, report, etc. that provides for a special supportive meeting with the teacher. It should not be a scheduled reprimand or negative meeting. This seems to be very effective because the student at first feels he is going to be criticized for something, which is customarily the reason for being asked to meet with the teacher. When given a compliment instead of a reprimand, his self-image will improve significantly! When his peers hear of this, they feel more comfortable when receiving a "See Me" slip. In fact, they look forward to having the opportunity for a one-on-one or small group positive interaction with the teacher. The teacher can also use this time to encourage growth in other areas; the student will be more receptive to this approach and more likely to freely express his concerns during this time rather than in a full traditional classroom environment. Student suggestions are enthusiastically received. This procedure is an excellent example of the *Motivational Theory* approach.

Positive Parent Communication
Middle and high school students are often reluctant to bring their parents to school for an "Open House" or a similar event. To change the negative connotation of parent meetings, call parents periodically to inform them about something their son or daughter is doing well in school. The idea is to share with the parents that you have *"Caught their child doing something good!"*

It's an enjoyable experience for both parent and teacher. The parent usually expects to hear the teacher complain and upon hearing a positive report, happily accepts the fact that it is not a complaint but rather a compliment! This will result in increased attendance during an Open House. The parents will make every effort to come in order to hear more about their children and meet the teacher face to face. It is even more impressive if the teacher can say something special about each child when the teacher gives his brief speech to those in attendance. He can have the parent's sign in as they arrive and then present some small positive comment about a child of the parent(s) in attendance for all to hear. When the parent arrives home, he will surely share this comment with pride with his child, which is a pleasant situation for all.

It is important that the classroom teacher is sensitive to the fact that many parents are frustrated by the change in behavior of their middle school and high school children. The once well-behaved child often adopts a new personality of rebellion or secrecy, and the parent is confused in regard to his actions and responses. Many schools have found success in offering parents an opportunity to attend parenting seminars. There are many available, such as "Effective Parenting," which provides descriptive sessions that can be led by the school guidance counselor.

In addition to concrete awards such as those presented here, intrinsic rewards reflect the basic concept of the *Motivational Theory*. Intrinsic rewards help students feel good about themselves by feeling pride in their work, knowing the importance of truth, and taking responsibility for their own actions. These are lessons well-learned.

The development of peer friendships among and between classmates is important. (See comments on *Cliques,* p. 133). Being part of a support system reinforces self-confidence. It shows clearly that we need each other to lead a mentally healthy and stable life. Seeing the teaching staff of a school working cooperatively together provides an excellent example for the students to follow. Secondary students need a support system that clearly defines right from wrong. At this age they typically experience many physical and social changes that make them feel disconnected, confused, and lonely. The teacher needs to be the role model. *His interaction with students should not use sarcasm, put-downs, ridicule, manipulation, or threats as a means of control of student behavior.*

The classroom needs to be a place that is fair to all students; this fair response to students is then reflected in the classroom organization. This organization should provide clearly stated rules of acceptable behavior. The teacher must show sensitivity by giving students the benefit of the doubt, providing uncomplicated directions throughout the class period, and being well-prepared so that the student can be comfortable with questions and errors that occur. As Barbara Striesand sings, *"Mistakes are lessons to be learned."* Each of us, as teachers, hopefully possesses these qualities and, by our example, consistently model the importance of responsibility toward one another, which will strengthen our own as well as our students' growth as persons of value.

E.   ACTING UPON THE TYPICAL INSECURITIES OF SELF AMONG ADOLESCENTS

Accepting the concept that pre-adolescent and adolescent students in middle and high school are building the bridges necessary to move into adulthood, the classroom teacher can most effectively communicate with these students by using the following standards. The standards help make the transition from a protected child to an independent adult much more successful.

- Be patient and listen to the student. Give him a time to talk and respond in an honest and sincere manner.

- Do not patronize him by saying such things as, "You'll appreciate that more when you are older." *Now* is the time the student wants to feel successful and accepted among his peers. Show your students the respect you would show any adult and expect the same from them. One high school teacher finds success in addressing all his students as "Mr. and "Ms."

- Within your teaching, show tolerance, acceptance and understanding of both right and wrong responses. Thus the student will feel more comfortable about trying. Show that the adult is not always right and the student always wrong during discussions. Listen to the rational for the student's responses. Teachers that listen learn something new everyday.

- Create an atmosphere and structure situations where the student can be made to feel valuable. Comment on how his contribution has enhanced the discussion. Encourage creativity and free thought.

- Admit when you are wrong.

- Accept your students' imperfections so that you and they are clearer about the direction in which they can grow to become more complete persons.

- It is important that the *criticism of the student by the teacher* deal clearly with what is wrong with the *behavior* and how it can be changed. Such criticism should be done privately to avoid embarrassing the student, which would negate any learning or positive reinforcement for change.

- Be sensitive of the daily crises that seem to be characteristic within an adolescent's life. Be tolerant of inconsistencies and moodiness.

- Never preach, lecture, or shout to make a point.

- Be supportive of the student's ideas and goals even if they appear to be unrealistic. It is the fact that the youngster is thinking and planning that is important (Stamm & Nissman, *Improving Middle School Guidance,* p. 29).

- Encourage with sincere enthusiasm the original thought or question. Let students know that questioning is the basis for learning and understanding new concepts and ideas.

- When a student responds in class, encourage him to enlarge and elaborate upon his answer. Follow this by requesting that other students to "piggy-back" on the original response with their ideas and questions. Stimulate class interaction by asking questions that cannot be answered with one thought— questions that have a variety of correct responses.

- *Support the concept that school is a place to learn and experience new ideas and concepts, rather than a place where rote learning exclusively takes place.*

- Acknowledge your students' participation and positive action by challenging their responses with thoughtful questions and comments.

F. THEORY SUMMARY

The *Motivational Theory* briefly presented here is very simplistic. It encourages the positive reinforcement of the students' acceptable behavior in the classroom, as well as in other areas of the school. The teacher, school and community encourage positive behavior by helping students feel worthy. This reward system provides the tools and suggestions to do just that. It also promotes the experience of gratification through success combined with encouragement and recognition of incentives to achieve and consequently develop a love of learning.

Achievement needs to be recognized by the teacher's acknowledging even the smallest display of positive behavior. That is the key. Typically, the exceptional students seems to receive all the awards, all the praise, and all the recognition on so many occasions; other students are often overlooked because their achievements are smaller and less dramatic. It is important that the average or slower student receives his share of positive recognition and encouragement. Each day every student should enter and/or leave each classroom feeling worthy and having known success. The successful use of this logical concept can make the difference between a classroom climate built for success and one that is stressful, negative, and likely to lead to failure.

The classroom teacher can build this environment through his enthusiasm and energy, by being well prepared for every lesson, by knowing his students, and by encouraging students' growth and development. These actions can help form a community of learners that can't wait until the next class session.

SECTION V

THE SCHOOL COUNSELOR'S ROLE IN CLASSROOM MANAGEMENT

THE SCHOOL COUNSELOR'S ROLE IN CLASSROOM MANAGEMENT

As we observe middle and high school students, we see them in the throes of change. New, undefined pressures can cause added stress to the conflicts already part of their life. As they move through school, they are asked to make decisions that may influence them dramatically for the rest of their lives. To help them make wise choices the school counselor is trained to assist in course decisions and future educational plans. Good counselors consider the whole child and provide a listening ear for their counselees as well as having a hand on the pulse of the school. The counselor is the sounding board for the classroom teacher, as well as a resource in communication skills and child development.

The counselor should provide the meeting place for the student and/or teacher that seeks him out. The effective counselor supports the students' fundamental need to assert his independence. This professional in the school community should be able to provide the expertise in human growth and development as a supportive service to teachers and parents in understanding the special needs of these preadolescent and adolescent students. As stated in Stamm and Nissman's *The Middle School Counselor*, the image of the counselor can be described succinctly through a well-known adage with a slight twist, "The I's have it!" The counselor's role demands *Intelligence, Information, Interest, Involvement, Initiative, Inquisitiveness, Inspiration and Indestructibility*" (p. 112). With these components intact, the counselor is there for the student and is capable of providing a support system vital to the classroom teacher and the student's parents, as well as to the individual student and students in group discussions of common concerns.

It is not unusual for the school counselor to have a very heavy caseload and cannot realistically spend a great deal of the school day meeting individually with students. Much of his time is spent on scheduling and extreme problems. It is therefore suggested that among the counseling staff, a proportion of time during the week be allotted for student direct interaction and that this time for personal counseling be clearly noted on each counselor's office door. Thus the student who has a problem can arrange time to meet with the counselor concerning matters other than class scheduling. Some counselors feel more comfortable than others working directly with student concerns. It would be wise for the counseling staff to encourage that person to be most available to the students.

In addition, it would be helpful for the director of the counseling staff to schedule counseling information sessions for classroom teachers during their scheduled workshop days. These meetings would respond to teacher concerns and provide effective general techniques and procedures in response to specific problems of adolescent students. It is even more helpful if the teachers submit a listing of their concerns beforehand, so that the counselor can directly address them at the meeting. Most schools have specialists on their staffs that meet only through classes or provide other services. It is very productive to have these staff members periodically present their role to the staff and how they can assist the classroom teacher most effectively.

It is also helpful for counselors to meet with parenting groups to respond to parent concerns regarding their children. Adolescence is a very difficult time for both parents and children. Any sources of help and suggestions are usually responded to with enthusiasm. (Refer to "Additional Resources" provided at the end of this booklet.)

SECTION VI

CONCLUSION AND ADDITIONAL RESOURCES

CONCLUSION

As you peruse the suggestions and information provided in this booklet, I hope that it makes a significant impact on the quality of your classroom climate.

It is important that each of us in the field of education realize that what we are today will be different tomorrow. The events that surround us modify our behavior as well as our professional and personal lives.

To grow as a person one should be sensitive to four basic concepts:

1. How much are we willing to invest in what we do?
2. What kinds of risks are we willing to take?
3. How willing are we to learn about ourselves and understand our own strengths and weaknesses?
4. What do we need to do to get where we want to go in life?

It is important to recognize that the *biggest room in any school is the room for improvement*. All of us need persons to reinforce us, to caution us, to think and plan with us; in turn we need to provide this support for our colleagues. That is the essence of this booklet. When working as part of a school faculty it can easily be observed that our colleagues span many years of age and experience. This should not deter us or separate us from them, as difference is not measured by age but by energy levels, philosophy, experiences, and the intensity of our desire to learn and grow. To provide a truly functional learning environment, all involved in the process must demonstrate their respect and confidence in one another. Although there is much that a teacher can do in his classroom, it cannot function as an isolated arena within the school. There is a need for a strong partnership among the teachers, the administration, parents of the students, the students, and the community itself.

The educational process needs to show sensitivity to the environment of the times in which we live. Changes in lifestyle and social philosophy are reflected in each new generation. It is said that children of the 21st century have been inoculated with vitamin I—"I need this, I need that." Instant gratification is the name of the game. But change is healthy when it is shared and enjoyed. We, as educators, learn much as we listen and observe, as well as when we begin to explore our responsibilities in the classroom. *The classroom provides us with a platform upon which we are able to present our best.* We should remember that students are far more alike than they are different; we need to understand them and become an integral part of their lives. We need to keep in mind that time is a gift we give ourselves and our students—time to think, time to discover, and time to relate what is learned to the changing world that surrounds us.

All of our students are not equally capable and often respond to different learning modalities. As sensitive teachers, we need to recognize these differences and allow our students and ourselves an opportunity for success. For this reason, the suggestions given in this booklet will be the answer for one student and not for another. The teacher needs to make the appropriate choice to react to the situation. *We must have the courage to step outside of the comfort zone and take risks that will challenge our students more than they have ever been challenged. We must trust our students so that they feel it is a supportive quality of trust. We must love our students whether they are bright or average, clean or slovenly, animated or shy.* Many of the students in our schools today have never been challenged, loved, or trusted! Their time in school may be the only time of sanity that they experience.

As classroom teachers we are our students' connection to a healthy personal development and positive self-image. As Dr. Spock once said, "If a child picks up a virus of failure and inferiority and exposure to neglect and negative attitudes about life between the ages of six to twelve, there is liable to be a fever in the teenage years."

We need to remember that *success comes before work only in the dictionary* so we need to realize that we can represent our profession well and properly by loving our work, laughing through those difficult moments, listening to those around us, and we will experience the world of wonderment—the excitement of making a difference in fulfilling our role as educators.

We must all become the kind of teacher that *looks forward rather than backward even though it may be easier to remember where you have been than to figure out where you are going.* As we keep in mind that childhood is a journey, not a race but rather a time to think, create, question, and reassess, we truly will have discovered the foundation for effective interaction with our students, which leads to productive and successful learning. *Great moments aren't judged on how long they last but how long they are remembered.* A student whom we have touched in support and trust will most likely remember the moment and cherish it.

As a teacher we have joined a community of responsible citizens. Our responsibility is to teach. In order to teach we must be able to manage our classroom climate effectively. We have been given the power and the responsibility to use our knowledge and our energy to make a difference. As we accept this mantel of professionalism, will we be among those professional educators who make school a place where both teachers and students want to be?

ADDITIONAL RESOURCES

Books

Arum, Richard. *Judging School Discipline: The Crisis of Moral Authority.* Cambridge, MA: Harvard University Press, 2003.

Avers, William , Bernardine Dohrn, and Rick Ayers: *Zero Tolerance: Resisting the Drive for Punishment in Our Schools: A Handbook for Parents, Students, Educators and Citizens.* New York: New Press: W.W. Norton, 2001.

Burden, Paul R. *Classroom Management and Discipline: Methods to Facilitate Cooperation and Instruction.* New York: Longman, 1995.

Beaudion, Marie-Nathalie, and Maureen Taylor. *Breaking the Culture of Bullying and Disrespect, Grades K-8: Best Practices and Successful Strategies.* Thousand Oaks, CA: Corwin Press, 2004.

Burden, Paul R. *Classroom Management; Creating a Successful Learning Community,* 2nd ed. New York: Wiley, 2003.

Burke, Kay. *What to Do With the Kid Who—,* 2nd Ed. Arlington Heights, Illinois: Skylight Professional Development, 2000.

Canter, Lee and Marlene Canter. *Assertive Discipline,* 3rd ed. Canter & Associates, 2002.

Cipani, Ennio. *Classroom Management for All Teachers: 12 Plans for Evidence-Based Practices,* 2nd ed. Upper Saddle River, NJ: Pearson/Merrill/Prentice Hall, 2004.

Coombs-Richardson, Rita, Charles H. Melsgeier, Carol Torrey. *Discipline Options: Establishing a Positive School Climate.* Norwood, MA: Christopher-Gordon Publishers, 2001.

Curwin, Richard I and Mendler, Allen N. *Discipline with Dignity.* Upper Saddle River, NJ: Merrill, 2001.

Dubelle, Stanley T. *Student Self Discipline: Helping Students Behave Responsibly.* Rockport, ME: ProActive Publications, 1995.

Dalbeck, Dr. Ruth. *Successful Child Discipline in Three Easy Steps,* LLC. Vision for Life Publishing Co. (*www.e-book*) format 2004.

Darch, Craig B and Edward J. Kameenul. *Instructional Classroom Management: A proactive Approach to Behavior Management, 2nded.* Columbus, Ohio: Prentice Hall, 2003.

Dreikurs, Rudolf, Pearl Cassel, and Eva Dreikurs-Ferguson: *Discipline Without Tears: how to reduce Conflict and Establish Cooperation in the Classroom.* Wiley, John & Sons, Inc., 2004.

Edwards, Clifford H. *Classroom Discipline and Management 4th ed.* New York: Wiley, 2004.

Goodlad, J.J., C. Mantle-Bromley, and S. J. Goodlad. *Education for Everyone: Agenda for Education in a Democracy.* San Francisco: Jossey-Bass, 2004.

Glasser, William. *Reality Therapy.* New York: Harper and Row, 1965.

Glasser, William. *Schools Without Failure.* New York: Harper and Row, 1975.

Gordon, Ann. *Guiding Young Children in a Diverse Society.* Boston: Allyn & Bacon, 1996.

Harmin, Merrill. *Inspiring Discipline: A Practical Guide for Today's Classrooms.* West Haven, CT: NEA Professional Library, 1995.

Hartwig, Eric Paul. *Discipline in the School,* 2nd ed. Horsham, PA: LRP Publications, 2001.

Jones, Vernon F. and Louise S. Jones. *Comprehensive Classroom Management: Creating Communities of Support and Solving Problems: 7th ed.* Boston: Allyn and Bacon, Inc, 2003.

Koenig, Larry. *Smart Discipline for the Classroom: Respect and Cooperation Restored,* 3rd ed. Thousand Oaks, California: Corwin Press 2004.

Kohn, Alfie. *Beyond Discipline: From Compliance to Community.* Alexandria, VA: ASCD, 1996.

Kosier, Ken. *Discipline checklist: Advice From 60 Successful Teachers.* Washington, D.C.: NEA Professional Library, 2002.

Mackenzie, Robert J. *Setting Limits in the Classroom: How to Move Beyond the Dance of Discipline in Today's Classrooms,* 2nd ed. Crown Publishing Group, 2003.

Nelson, Jane, Lynn Lott, H. Stephen Glenn. *Positive Discipline in the Classroom: Developing Mutual Respect, Cooperation, and Responsibility in Your Classroom.* Three Rivers Press, 2000.

Nelson, Jane, Roslyn Duffy, Debbie Owen-Sohocki, Linda Escobar, Kate Ortolano. *Positive Discipline; A Teacher's A-Z Guide: Hundreds of Solutions for Almost*

Every Classroom Behavior Problem! 2nd ed. Crown Publishing Group (Positive Discipline Series), 2001.

Perro, Ann. *Talk it Out: Conflict Resolution in the Elementary Classroom.* Alexandria, VA: ASCD, 1996.

Phelan, Thomas W, Sarah Jane Scheneur, and Dan Farrell (Illustrator). *Management for Teachers: Effective Classroom Discipline, Pre-K Through Grade 8.* Parentmagic, Inc, 2004.

Ross, Dorothea M. *Childhood Bullying and Teasing: What School Personnel, Other Parents and Personnel Can Do.* Alexandria, VA: American Counseling Association, 1996.

Senge, Peter M, Timothy Lucas, Bryan Smith, Janis Dutton, and Nelda Cambron-McCabe. *Schools That Learn: A Fifth Discipline Fieldbook for Educators, Parents, and Everyone Who Cares About Education.* Doubleday & Company, Inc., 2000.

Shingles, Beryl and Norma Lopez-Reyna. *Cultural Sensitivity in the Implementation of Discipline Policies and Practices.* Arlington, VA: Council for Children with Behavioral Disorders; Council of Administrators of Special Education, 2002.

Stamm, Martin L., and Blossom S. Nissman. *Improving Middle School Guidance.* Boston, Massachusetts: Allyn and Bacon Inc, 1979.

Tomlinson. C.A. *How to Differentiate Instruction in Mixed-Ability Classrooms,* 2nd edition. Alexandria, VA.: ASCD, 2001.

Wasley, P.A., R.I. Hampel, and R.W. Clark. *Kids and School Reform.* San Francisco: Kossey-Bass, 1997.

Van Acker, Richard. *Establishing and Monitoring a School and Classroom Climate that Promotes Desired Behavior and Academic Achievement.* Arlington, VA: Council for Children with Behavioral Disorders; Council of Administrators of Special Education, 2002.

Wielkiewicz, Richard M. *Behavior Management in the Schools: Principles and Procedures,* 2nd ed. Boston: Allyn & Bacon, 1995.

Walker, Hill M and Michael H Epstein. *Making Schools Safer and Violence Free: Critical Issues, Solutions, and Recommended Practices.* Austin, Texas, Pro-Ed, 2001.

Walker, Hill M., Elizabeth Ramsey and Frank M Gresham. *Antisocial Behavior in School: Evidence-Based Practices,* 2nd ed. Belmont, CA: Thomson/Wadsworth. 2004.

Wolfgang, Charles H. *Solving Discipline Problems: Methods & Models for Today's Teachers,* 3rd edition. Boston: Allyn & Bacon, 1995.

Wells, Hillary, Susan K. Lewis, Dick Bartlett, and David Ly. *Survivor's Guide* (television series) PBS: 2004.

Wolfgang, Charles H. *Solving Discipline and Classroom Management Problems: Methods and Models for Today's Teachers,* 6th ed. Wiley, John & Sons, Inc., 2004.

Periodicals

Algozzine, Robert, Audette, Robert, Ellis, Edward. *Teaching Exceptional Children,* "Supporting teachers, principals and students through unified discipline." Vol. 33, No.2 (November/December 2000) pp. 42-47.

Casella, Ronnie. *Teachers College Record*: "Zero Tolerance Policy in School; Rationale, Consequences and Alternatives. Vol. 105 No. 5 (June 2003) pp. 872-92.

Denton, Paula. *American Secondary Education,* "Shared Rule-Making in Practice: The Jefferson Communities at Kingston High School." Vol. 31 No. 3 (Summer 2003), pp. 66-96.

Effrat, Andrew, Schimmel, David. *American Secondary Education,* "Walking the Democratic Talk: Introduction to a Special Issue on Collaborative Rule-Making as Preparation for Democratic Citizenship." Vol. 31, No. 3 (Summer 2003), pp. 32-15.

George, Heather Peshak, Harrower, Joshua K, Knoster, Tim. *Preventing School Failure,* "School Wide Prevention and Early Intervention: A Process for Establishing a System of School-Wide Behavior Support." Vol. 47, No 4 (Summer 2003), pp. 170-6.

Grandmont, Richard P. *American Secondary Education,* "Judicious Discipline: A Constitutional Approach for Public High Schools." Vol. 31 No. 3 (Summer 2003) pp. 97-117.

Hinchey, Patricia H. *The Clearing House,* "Corporal Punishment: Legalities, Realities and Implications." Vol. 77 No. 3 (January/February 2004), pp. 96-100.

Mayer, Roy G, *Education and Treatment of Children,* "Antisocial Behavior: Its Causes and Prevention Within Our Schools." Volume 24 No. 4 (November 2001), pp. 412-429.

Rosenberg, Michael S., Jackman. Lon A. *Intervention in School and Clinic,* "Development, Implementation, and Sustainability of Comprehensive School-Wide Behavior Management Systems." Vol. 39 No. 1 (September 2003), pp. 10-21.

Schimmel, David. *American Secondary Education,* "Collaborative Rule-Making and Citizenship Education: An Antidote to the Undemocratic Hidden Curriculum." Vol. 31, No. 3, (Summer 2003) pp. 16-35.

Schutz, Aaron. *Educational Researcher,* "Rethinking Domination and Resistance; Challenging Postmodernism." Vol. 33, No. 1 (January/February 2004), pp. 15-23.

Sprague, Jeffrey, Walker, Hill, Golly, Annemieke. *Education and Treatment of Children,* "Translating Research Into Effective Practice: The Effects of a Universal Staff and Student Intervention on Indicators of Discipline and School Safety." Vol. 24, No. 4 (November 2001), pp. 495-511.

Sciba, Russell J, Peterson, Reece. *Preventing School Failure,* "Teaching the Social Curriculum: School Discipline as Instruction." Vol. 47 No. 2 (Winter 2003), pp. 66-73.

White, Richard, Algozzine, Robert, Audette, Robert. *Intervention in School and Clinic,* "Unified Discipline: A School-Wide Approach for Managing Problem Behavior." Vol. 37, No. 1 (September 2001), pp. 3-8.